Happy EATING

4/9/68

Recipes
from Irish Country Houses

By Gillian Berwick

Illustrated by Jeremy Williams

I wish to express my indebtedness to the many owners of the hotels and restaurants as well as friends and colleagues who have given me their time, assistance and encouragement to produce the material for this book.

First published in 1987 by Berwick Publishers.

Printers-Blacks of Cavan, Ireland.

Copyright,
ISBN 0 9511612 10.

Editor Rita Corrie.

Cookery Consultant — Myrtle Allen.

Wholly designed, set up and printed in Ireland.

By the same author —
"Making your own Chocolates".

Foreword.

Gillian Berwick was brought up in Australia, but she travelled the world several times during her teens, with her family, on business trips, invariably staying at famous hotels wherever they went.

After college Gillian studied cookery and went into business in this field in Australia.

In 1985 she decided to further her cookery studies in Ireland, and was later joined by her parents. They took apartments in one of the great private country houses of the Midlands. The house and the cookery school made a double impression on Gillian, so she had this good idea of presenting, in book form, the food and buildings of the present-day large country house in Ireland. She chose houses which are open to the public and are grouped together in a single organisation which accepts only those with the highest standards– the Irish Country House and Restaurant Association. Here she found a new dimension in the world of hotels.

Jeremy Williams, the architect and artist who is most closely associated with the restoration and maintenance of these houses, travelled the country with her to illustrate this book. Nobody more than Jeremy cares for or can capture the charm that makes each house unique and individual. There is no streaming into a marketable uniformity here, simply individuals in their own homes, free to equip, decorate and run their premises as they choose, and to share it with those who want a real glimpse of Ireland.

The only obligatory standards they must share is a high degree of comfort and service to provide a good table. You will see that this is no cottage cookery book, the occupants of "the big house" have always served sophisticated food and known how to adapt new recipes from abroad to the good Irish ingredients. In this case each recipe has been left virtually as the owner or his chef contributed it. If you are puzzled with one– write to the house directly, or better still, pay a visit and taste it there!

Myrtle Allen.
Ballymaloe House,
Shanagarry,
Co. Cork.
May, 1987.

Introduction

I rish country houses have always had one thing in common—hospitality is paramount. In Ireland, this tradition goes back to ancient times when the traveller, bard or stranger was watched for and welcomed as one who carried tidings from far and wide. When he arrived he was the centre and focus of attention, to be served with the best while he gave his news. Whether the country house was a castle or a mansion, a priory or a cottage, the reaction was the same. This in part, explains the special welcome received by visitors to the Irish Country House Hotels and Restaurants.

Throughout the centuries, Ireland has exported people like the Swiss today export "Swatches". All over the globe, in America, Australia, Canada, people have "come from" Ireland. My interest in Irish country houses blossomed when I came to Ireland from Australia— a Swatch in reverse! and began living in one. I became obsessed with history, styles and periods. I automatically looked up at the ceiling when I walked into a strange room, admiring the craftmanship of some past artisan. I mused about the great Irish literary figures of the past, from Goldsmith, Swift and Moore to Yeats and Shaw and wondered how many had graced these rooms.

Being a cookery writer, however, my enthusiasm finally focused on the kitchens and I wanted to share my experiences of Irish Country House Hotels with all who visit or return searching for a taste of Ireland.

From times past the country houses have always had their walled gardens for fruit and vegetables, well stocked greenhouses and a bountiful supply of fresh herbs. Pickles, jams and other preserves were made and stored, but vegetables were, of necessity, always served according to what was "in season". As this tradition, thankfully, remains, I have omitted vegetables from most menus.

I am grateful for the enthusiasm with which my proposal to write an Irish country house cookbook was received by the proprietors. I have been given first hand experience of their Irish hospitality and can vouch for the professionalism of their enterprises and the acclaimed cuisine for which many of them have won prestigious international awards.

These are not my own recipes, but contributions generously given to me to use in my book by the individual chefs of the I.C.H.R.A.

Gillian Berwick,
Emo Court,
Emo, Co. Laois.

Contents

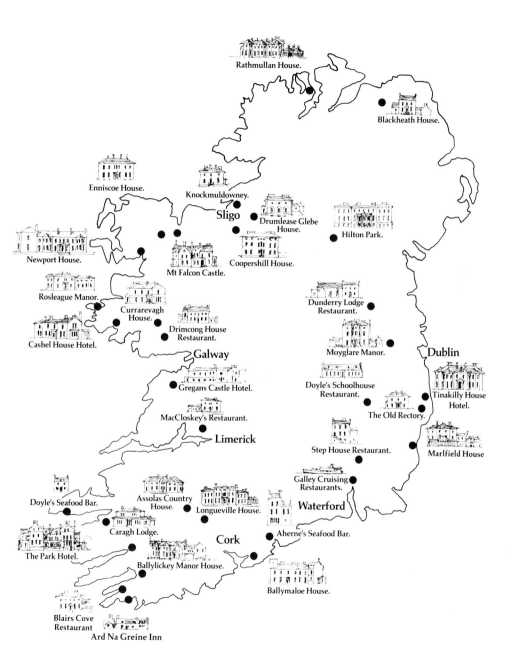

Rathmullan House.

Blackheath House.

Enniscoe House.

Knockmuldowney.

Sligo

Drumlease Glebe House.

Hilton Park.

Newport House.

Coopershill House.

Mt Falcon Castle.

Rosleague Manor.

Currarevagh House.

Dunderry Lodge Restaurant.

Cashel House Hotel.

Drimcong House Restaurant.

Moyglare Manor.

Dublin

Galway

Gregans Castle Hotel.

Doyle's Schoolhouse Restaurant.

Tinakilly House Hotel.

MacCloskey's Restaurant.

The Old Rectory.

Limerick

Step House Restaurant.

Marlfield House

Galley Cruising Restaurants.

Doyle's Seafood Bar.

Assolas Country House.

Longueville House.

Waterford

Caragh Lodge.

Aherne's Seafood Bar.

The Park Hotel.

Cork

Ballylickey Manor House.

Ballymaloe House.

Blairs Cove Restaurant

Ard Na Greine Inn

Old Rectory

L inda and Paul Saunders run the lovely "Old Rectory" hotel-restaurant in its tranquil garden setting just outside the harbour town of Wicklow. It has a small, pleasant restaurant, candle-lit and in the cooler evenings, a great log fire. Not surprisingly being situated near the sea, fish is a speciality and is served, as is all the food, with great individuality. Salmon, lobster, crab and sea trout are fresh from the sea. There are other interesting things like chicken with cream cheese and grapes in puff pastry, on the menu and to finish off you can have your "Swan Lake", the result of Linda's wizardry with the piping bag.

Bedrooms are colourful, tastefully furnished and well equipped. You can choose an Irish, Swiss, or Scottish breakfast to start your day. County Wicklow, one of the lovliest counties in Ireland is waiting outside to be explored.

The Old Rectory,
Wicklow,
Co. Wicklow.

This ex-rectory was built in 1875 and has been converted into a small hotel/restaurant. The style is Victorian, typical of the domestic architecture of Irish country rectories, with marble fire places, white in the lounge and black in the dining room, a customary arrangement for old rectories—wedding parties to one room and funeral parties to another!

9

Potato and Ham Soup.

2 pints (1.150 litres)/5 cups ham stock, (not too salty).
1 lb (450 grams)/3 cups potatoes (peeled and chopped roughly)
1 large onion, (peeled and chopped roughly).
4 bay leaves.
2 tblspns cooked ham, (chopped).
1 tblspn fresh chives or spring onion tops, (chopped).
Salt and freshly ground black pepper.
2 oz (55 grams)/¼ cup cream.

Bring the first four ingredients to the boil and simmer until the potatoes are tender. Remove bay leaves and liquidize until smooth. Bring back to the boil and simmer for 2 minutes. Add the chopped ham and chives; adjust the seasoning according to your taste. (If a slightly richer taste is desired, stir in one teaspoon of brandy and one teaspoon of butter). Serve in warmed soup bowls topped with a teaspoon of whipped cream and a tiny pinch of nutmeg.

Crab Claws Malibu.

The mouth watering sweetness of freshly cooked crab claws makes us wonder why lobster is so highly thought of. We use the claws of Kilmore Quay crabs and crack all of the outside shell, except the pincer, to make them easier to eat. Enthusiastic diners will inevitably finish up by dipping the claws in the delicious sauce with their fingers, so provide a finger bowl of luke warm water with thin slices of lemon floating on top.

36 large cooked crab claws (with shell removed).
1 pint (600 ml)/2½ cups well flavoured fish stock.
1 oz (30 grams)/¼ cup dessicated coconut.
3 oz (85 grams)/6 tblspns butter.
2 oz (55 grams)/¾ cup flour.
4 oz (110 grams)/1¼ cups button mushrooms (washed and quartered).
4 oz (110 grams)/2/3 cup diced fresh pineapple.
4 fl. oz (120 ml)/½ cup double cream.
2 fl. oz (60 ml)/¼ cup 'Malibu' coconut liqueur.
Salt and cayenne pepper.

Place crab claws in one layer in buttered ovenproof serving dish. Dot with 1 oz (30 grams)/2 tblspns butter, cover with foil and heat through at 300°F/150°C/Regulo 2 for 25 minutes. Melt 2 oz (55 grams)/4 tblspns butter in a pan, blend in flour, cook over low heat for 2-3 minutes, stirring constantly with a wooden spoon. Add the warmed fish stock gradually, beating all the time so that the sauce stays smooth, and bring to the boil. Simmer for 5 minutes. Add coconut, mushrooms, pineapple and cream. Heat through, but do not boil. Add salt and a pinch of cayenne pepper to taste. Finally, blend in the coconut liqueur and pour immediately over the crab claws. Toss gently to coat all claws in sauce and incorporate any spare butter.

To serve: Decorate with trimmed pineapple leaves and cucumber 'fans'. Green vegetables or a salad make a good accompaniment.

"Swan Lake" meringues.

We were looking for a memorable and beautiful shape in which to pipe meringues (having previously made baskets, shamrocks, baroque shapes etc) when I read the Irish folk tale 'The Singing Swans'. These meringues are the result. Our diners are so thrilled when they see them that they have often rushed for their cameras to take photographs! The basic meringue shapes are made in advance and assembled just before serving. They are a bit fragile to handle but well worth the effort. Any colours could be used but we find this combination of pale pink meringue and fresh green fruit particularly pleasing.

Whisk 4 egg whites until stiff and dry. Add 4 oz (110 grams)/½ cup granulated sugar and whisk at full speed for 30 seconds. Add 4 oz (110 grams)/½ cup sieved castor sugar and whisk only until combined. Add 2 drops peppermint essence and 1 drop red food colouring whisking lightly until just blended in. (N.B. Use a spoon, not the bottle). Take 3 flat baking trays, 16" by 12". (30.5 cm by 40.5 cm), cover in aluminium foil, then lightly grease all three. Using a piping bag and a star nozzle pipe 8 'bases', 16 'wings', and (on the foil covered tray), 10 'necks' (i.e. 8 plus 2 for breakages) as shown.

(If you have any spare mixture make a few stars and sprinkle with cocoa powder or stud with flaked almonds for 'petit fours' on a future occasion). Bake for 3 hours at 150°F/70°C/ Reg ⅛. When cooked, remove trays from oven, release 'necks' by peeling away foil (very carefully indeed) and release 'bases' and 'wings' by gently flexing trays. When cool, store in an airtight box (for up to 3 months). If any of the shapes begin to break, keep the pieces. They can be invisibly mended with a dab of cream at time of assembly.

To serve: Whip ½ pint (300 ml)/1¼ cups cream until stiff. Stick 'base' to serving plate with a dab of cream, place a heaped tblspn of cream on top, stick 'wings' one each side and 'neck' into the cream, centre front. Arrange green fruits, e.g. sliced kiwi fruits or halved, de-seeded green grapes around the swan to represent the lake, and fill back of swan with soft fruits such as strawberries or prepared pieces of chocolate. The final effect is enhanced by a small fresh flower and a larger sized under plate covered with a doyley.

pipe 8 'bases'   ... 16 'wings'   ... 10 'necks'
                                                (on the foil covered tray)

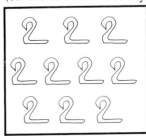

assemble like this:-

Tinakilly House was built in 1870 for Captain Halpin who laid the first telegraph cable across the Atlantic as Commander of the "Great Eastern". His architect was James Franklin Fuller and it is one of his best works. The most imposing space is the double height staircase hall designed as a central living room.

Tinakilly House

Four poster beds, log fires and period furniture make this a warm mature hotel for those who like peace and quiet. A sea farer's home par excellence, from the odd porthole window with a view of the sea to the majestic bathroom (happily kept intact) with its giant mahogany mounted bath, marble basin and throne-like loo, in all their Victorian glory, in front of a roaring fire. Stately reception rooms invite you to contemplate, congregate or just sit and sip your port after dinner in splendid seaman-like comfort. Bee and William Power have certainly earned full marks for furnishing and decorating the house in correct Victorian style.

Tinakilly House Hotel,
Rathnew,
Co. Wicklow.

Pigeon Breast Gelée.

2 pints (1 litre)/5 cups consommé made from chicken, pigeon or pheasant.
8 leaves gelatine.
½ lettuce.
½ raddichio lettuce.
½ head salade frisée, (curly lettuce).
3 pigeons.
3 shallots.
Butter for frying.
12 peeled tomatoes.
Chives, parsley, basil.
1 clove garlic, crushed.
Salt and pepper.
1 carrot.
1 courgette.
1 tomato, peeled and seeded.
French Dressing.

Make a consommé with chicken/pigeon/pheasant stock. Add 8 leaves of gelatine per 2 pints (1 litre)/5 cups. Cool down. Slice thinly a breast of pigeon and arrange nicely on one third of a serving plate. Finely chop 2 shallots and cook gently without browning in a little butter or oil until softened. Add 4 peeled, chopped tomatoes, 1 tspn each of chives, parsley and basil, 1 clove crushed garlic and seasoning. Cook slowly for 30 minutes and keep warm. Decorate pigeon breast with julienne strips of carrot, courgette and tomato. Glaze by spooning repeated coatings of gelatine mixture over the decorated breast. Decorate remainder of plate with lettuce and tomato mixture dressed with French Dressing.

Lamb in a Basil Sauce 'aux petits legumes'.

1 leg lamb.
2 tblspns olive oil and 5 oz (140 grams)/⅝ cup butter.
Salt and pepper.
2-3 sprigs basil.
2 shallots.
3 carrots.
3 turnips.
2 tblspns white wine.
1 pint (600 ml)/2½ cups veal stock.
4 fl. oz (125 ml)/¼ cup mushroom juice.
Parsley.

Fry lamb in a pan in the oil and ½ oz (15 grams)/1 tblspn of the butter. Season it with salt, pepper and 1 tspn of finely chopped basil. Place on a rectangle of tin foil large enough to wrap the joint in. Bake until cooked through, approx. 1½-2 hours at 400°F/200°C/Reg 6. Meanwhile cut shallots, carrots and turnips into the size of large olives and fry in the pan in the same oil and butter provided it is not burnt. Add a drop of white wine and more fresh basil and reduce. Add veal stock and mushroom juice. Reduce again by half. Enrich with some more butter. When the lamb is cooked place it on its serving dish and decorate it with parsley: serve the sauce separately.

Individually Cooked Apple Tarts.

Take one eating apple (per person). Peel and core. Slice at base so the apple will sit firmly, maintaining the apple shape. Place a marzipan finger in place of core. Place on a 3 inch (8 cm) diameter, ¼ inch (6 mm) thick, circle of short crust pastry. Cook at 400°F/200°C/Reg 6 for 20 minutes. Dust over with dry icing sugar and serve on a large plate with a mango and raspberry coulis.

Mango and Raspberry Coulis.

is made by liquidising the fruit and straining out pips. Sweeten the purée to taste. Mangoes must be peeled and stoned.

Marlfield House
"A very agreeable Place"

Those who love the old and mature will appreciate Marlfield House. Furniture and decoration are perfect. The bedrooms are spacious and elegant. The food is plentiful and expertly cooked. The 23,150 acre estate has shrunk to 35 acres. A previous visitor (in 1776) wrote this description of the landscape which is quite fitting today.

"Courtown is an agreeable place, and in some respects a very singular one, for the house is within 600 yards of the sea, and yet is almost buried in fine woods which from their growth and foliage show no aversion to their neighbours, who is so often pernicious to all their brethren. His (Lord Courtown's) views of the sea are fine, everywhere broken by wood or hilly varied ground. All his environs consist of undulating lands, which give a pleasant variety to the scene; a river enters his garden, and pursuing for some distance a sequested course, shaded on one side by a rocky bank, well wooded, and on the other by lofty trees, with a very agreeable walk under them, pours itself into the sea at a small distance from the house".

Marlfield
Gorey,
Co. Wexford.

Two mansions existed originally on the Courtown estate–"Courtown House" and its Dower House (Marlfield today). The former was the grander house with an estate of 23,150 acres which supported a lifestyle of great luxury and entertainment on a grand scale. Following the Irish famine of 1845-1849, when rent revenue dropped appreciably, like many of the mansions of its day, Courtown became very delapidated and was eventually demolished in 1948. The Dower House (Marlfield) became the principal residence in Ireland of the Courtown's until it was acquired by the Bowe family in 1979.

Salade de Pigeon.

Walnut Vinaigrette.
2 pigeon breasts.
(marinated overnight in; olive oil, garlic, orange zest, shallot, black pepper).
Curly endive.
Raddichio lettuce.
Oak leaf lettuce.
Fine, crispy garlic croutons.
2 oz (55 grams)/2 rashers of bacon.
Finely sliced white mushrooms.

Make a salad of the three types of lettuce, gently coated in the vinaigrette, alternating the colours of leaves. In a pan sauté the seasoned pigeon breasts for about 4 minutes. Remove from heat and allow to relax. Fry the bacon and mushrooms quickly in hot fat until crispy. Add to dish with pigeon breasts. Allow to absorb pigeon juices; then sprinkle bacon and mushrooms on salad. Finely carve the pink breasts and arrange attractively on the salad. Sprinkle with a few croutons and serve immediately.

Darne de Saumon aux Pointes d'Asperges.

2 middle cut steaks of wild salmon.
12 spears of asparagus.
Fish stock.
½ oz (15 ml) cream.
1 oz (30 grams)/2 tblspns butter.
Chives, finely chopped.
Chervil.

Place the prepared asparagus in enough boiling seasoned water to cover. Add some fresh chervil and a knob of butter. Cook until tender. Place the salmon in a shallow pan of boiling fish stock. Cover and place in a moderate oven until just cooked. Remove the fish and keep warm. Boil the liquor until only 2 tblspns remain. Add cream and butter and beat vigorously to bind the sauce. Add the chives at the last moment. Arrange the asparagus on the plate with the salmon. Coat with warm sauce. Serve immediately.

Tarte au Citron.

1½ lb (675 grams) shortbread dough.
14 oz (370 grams)/1¾ cups castor sugar.
Pinch of flour.
10fl. oz (300 ml)/1¼ cups cream.
4 lemons.
9 eggs.

To make shortbread.

8 oz (225 grams)/1 cup butter.
4 oz (110 grams)/¾ cup icing sugar.
2 egg yolks.
10 oz (285 grams)/1¼ cups flour.
Pinch salt.
Drop of vanilla or lemon essence.

Cut the butter into short pieces and place it on a wooden surface. Work the butter with your fingertips until it is very soft. Sift the icing sugar and add it to the butter with a pinch of salt. Work the mixture, still with fingertips, until the ingredients are thoroughly blended, then add the egg yolks and lightly mix all the ingredients together. Sift the flour and using your right hand amalgamate it evenly into the mixture. When the pastry is thoroughly mixed, add the vanilla or lemon essence. Rub the pastry two or three times using the palm of your hand but do not over-work it. Roll it into a ball and flatten it out lightly. Wrap in greaseproof paper and chill for several hours.

Pastry Base.

Pre-heat oven to 325°F/160°/Regulo 3. On a lightly floured wooden surface, roll out the pastry to about 1/6 inch (4mm) thick. Butter a flan ring 9 inch (25 cm) diameter, 1½ inches (4 cm) deep. Place on a buttered baking sheet and line with the pastry. Put a circle of greaseproof paper in the bottom, fill with dried beans and bake in preheated oven for 10 minutes. Remove from the oven, take out the beans and paper and keep the pastry shell at room temperature. Lower the oven temperature to 300°F (150°C)/Reg 2.

The Lemons.

Wash, grate the zests and squeeze the lemons, reserving the zests and juice together.

The Eggs.

Break them into a bowl, add the sugar and beat lightly with a wire whisk until the mixture is smooth and well blended.

The Cream.

Pour the cream onto the egg mixture and beat very lightly with a wire whisk. Stir in the lemon juice and zests and pour the filling onto the pastry case.

Cooking.

Place immediatly in the pre-heated oven and cook for 40 minutes. If the top of the tart becomes too brown before the end of the cooking time, cover with foil. When the tart is cooked, remove the flan ring before it cools completely.

The history of the original castle (of which part remains) dates back to 1450. Built by the Fitzgerald family, it was held by them until 1641, when it passed to Lord Broghill who entertained both William Penn and Cromwell at Ballymaloe. Changing hands many times during the 17th, 18th and 19th centuries, it passed to Ivan Allen in 1948 and became an hotel in 1967.

Ballymaloe House

Ballymaloe House has always been synonymous with great cooking. In County Cork where international award winning restaurants abound, it is in good company. Much of the food comes from the Allen family farms and the fish from neighbouring fishing villages. The family enterprises also include a craft shop, farm shop and cookery school. The hotel has 30 bedrooms in the main building and courtyard. Ivan Allen is the family wine buff and Myrtle responsible for the wizardry in the kitchen. A benign ghost called Chuff (a dwarf) is said to haunt the old castle but he doesn't seem to ruffle the tranquility of Ballymaloe House in Shanagarry.

Ballymaloe House,
Shanagarry,
Midleton,
Co. Cork.

Lettuce and Mint Soup.

4 oz (110 grams)/1 cup peeled diced onions.
5 oz (140 grams)/1 cup chopped potatoes.
1 tspn salt.
Freshly-ground pepper.
6 oz (170 grams)/3 cups chopped lettuce leaves.
2 pints (1.2 litres)/5 cups stock.
2 tspns freshly chopped mint.
1 tblspn cream, (optional).
2 oz (55 grams)/4 tblspns butter.

Melt butter in a heavy saucepan. When it foams, add potatoes and onions and turn them until well coated. Sprinkle with salt and pepper. Cover and sweat on a gentle heat for 10 minutes. Add chopped lettuce leaves and stock. Boil until soft. Liquidise, sieve or put through a mouli. Do not overcook or the vegetables will lose their flavour. Adjust seasoning. Add mint and cream.
Note: Good for using the coarse outer leaves of the lettuce, or a head that is starting to wilt or shoot.

Lamb Roast with Irish Garden Herbs.

5 lb (2.25 kilo) joint of lamb.
2 tblspns good quality oil.
2 cloves garlic.
1 tblspn each of the following herbs chopped & mixed in even amounts.
Parsley, thyme, chives, marjoram, mint, tarragon.
1 level tspn finely chopped rosmary.
1 extra tspn each of these herbs for the sauce.
8 fl. oz (250 ml)/1 cup stock.

Prepare a paste of the oil, garlic and herbs. Peel and crush garlic in a little salt and blend with the oil. Mix in the chopped herbs. Sprinkle the lamb with salt and pepper and rub in the herb mixture. The lamb can be left to stand in this mixture for up to 24 hours, or can be roasted right away.

Preheat oven to 400°F/200°C/Reg 6. Roast lamb for approximately 1½ to 1¾ hours, when it should still be slightly pink in the middle. Test with a skewer, the juices should run out pink. Remove lamb and place on a warm serving dish. Meanwhile spoon off the surplus fat from the roasting pan. Add the herbs and stock to the cooking juices. Boil up, scraping the pan well and serve separately in a sauce boat.

Irish Mist Soufflé.

10-14 lemons.
4 eggs
1 large sweet geranium leaf (Pelargonium Graveolens).
1 tblspn Irish Mist.
4 tblspns castor sugar.
2 small lemons.
2 tspns gelatine.

This mixture can be filled into lemon skins or served as a soufflé. If filling lemons, cut the tops off, scoop out the insides and strain. Otherwise squeeze lemons in the ordinary way. Crush the geranium leaf in your hand and put it in the lemon juice. Beat egg yolks with sugar to a thick mousse using an electric mixer or by hand over a saucepan of boiling water. Add Irish Mist and beat again. Put gelatine, 2 tspns of lemon juice and 1 tblspn of water in a pyrex or china bowl. Place this in a saucepan of water, making sure it doesn't touch the base of the saucepan. Bring the water to the boil. Do not stir but let simmer until the gelatine has dissolved. Blend gelatine and remaining strained lemon juice with the mousse. Put the geranium leaf in too, if you think enough flavour has not been extracted. Beat egg whites stiff and fold in. The sweet should be served semi-frozen.

The soufflé: These quantities make 2 pints (1.2 litres)/5 cups in volume, enough to fill a 1½ pint (900 ml) soufflé dish. Greaseproof paper should be tied round the soufflé dish to give it another 2 inches (5 cm) in height. You then over fill the dish, freeze for 4 hours and remove the paper. Top with a rosette of whipped cream and a large geranium leaf.

The Lemons: Fill lemon skins with the mixture and freeze for 4 hours. You will have lemon pulp left over which can be strained and used for some other purpose.

Ard na Greine Inn.

Ard na Greine Inn in Schull is a rather special place– warm, friendly and helpful in a very charming way. It has a tranquil almost sub-tropical (it has the benefit of the Gulf Stream) garden and terraces, overlooking the Fastnet Lighthouse. The fully licensed restaurant has an impressive and varied menu– the fish dishes are quite superb. It is well situated for touring the picturesque mountain and lake country of West Cork or you can stay put in these idyllic surroundings. The bedrooms are tastefully furnished and very comfortable.

This corner of Cork and adjacent Co. Kerry is undoubtedly one of the most scenic areas of Europe. It abounds with clean, magnificent scenery. Narrow valleys, soft purple peaks, rocky crags, little waterfalls, lakes and mountain passes: roads where you can stop every few miles to gaze as another scenic view unfolds before you and not a bulldozer in sight!

Ard na Gréine Inn,
Schull,
Co. Cork.

Two early 18th century cottages, farm house and a barn have been converted into charming linked cottages and turned into an inn and restaurant by Frank and Rhona O'Sullivan.

Crab au Gratin.

1 lb (450 grams) fresh white crab meat.
4 medium sized fillets sole.
8 fl. oz (250 ml)/1 cup dry cider.
2 tspns white wine vinegar.
1 tspn anchovy essence.
½ tspn ground nutmeg.
2 oz (55 grams)/4 tblspns melted butter.
4 oz (110 grams)/1 cup white breadcrumbs.
2 oz (55 grams)/½ cup grated cheese.

Place skinned fish fillets in a greased ovenproof dish. Mix cider, vinegar, anchovy essence, and nutmeg together, season with salt and freshly ground black pepper. Pour over fish and place in a pre-heated oven 400°F/200°C/Reg 6 for 15-20 minutes. When ready mix the fish, crab meat, melted butter and ½ the breadcrumbs. Grease 6 scallop shells with butter, fill each with crab mixture, sprinkle with breadcrumbs and knobs of butter. Return to oven for 20 minutes, remove and sprinkle with grated cheese and place under a very hot grill until cheese is melted. Garnish and serve with lemon wedges.

Roast Leg of Lamb with Coriander Sauce.

1 medium leg of lamb.
2-3 cloves of garlic, crushed.
2 heaped tblspns of crushed coriander seeds.
1 glass of port.

Make 8-10 incisions on the meat. Put a small mixture of combined garlic & coriander into each incision. Place lamb on a meat rack in a roasting tin (no fat necessary) and give it 30 minutes at 450°F/230°C/Reg 8, then lower to 350°F/180°C/Reg 4-5 and cook for 30 minutes to the pound. When cooked, remove lamb and let it stand in a warm place. Tip off excess fat from roasting tin and add port to make a gravy. Carve and serve with redcurrant jelly.

Mango Ice-Cream.

½ pint (300 ml)/1 cup fresh mango purée.
Juice of 1 lime.
8 oz (225 grams)/1 cup castor sugar.
4 tblspns water.
¾ pint (450 ml)/1½ cups double cream.
Cream of tartar.

Put sugar and water into a saucepan. Add a pinch of cream of tartar, bring to boil over a low heat and stir until mixture thickens. Remove from stove and stir in mango purée and lemon juice. Allow to cool, then stir in lightly whipped cream until well blended. Place mixture in container and freeze. Serve with slices of fresh lime and langue-du-chat biscuits.

Built some 300 years ago, as a shooting lodge, by Lord Kenmare and extended by the Franco-Irish Graves family in 1950. Partially destroyed by a fire in 1984, it has now been restored to its original pre-1950 appearance.

Ballylickey Manor House

The manor house in the picturesque village of Ballylickey is in a formal park-like garden laid out along a river bank with sweeping vistas of Bantry Bay beyond, an area so beautiful, that it has been praised in ballad, song and poetry for many centuries. There is a cluster of very attractive chalets and a grade A licensed restaurant surrounding a swimming pool in one part of the garden. The newly restored manor house contains more formal, ample and stylish suites most of which have the photogenic view. The grounds were designed by George Graves' mother Kitty and contain a flooded rock garden. The house has mementoes of her brother-in-law, the poet, Robert Graves. The bright and sparkling interior decoration is the work of the present Mrs. Graves.

Ballylickey Manor House,
Bantry Bay,
Co. Cork.

Piccatas of Duck, Liver Foie Gras.

21 oz (600 grams) Duck Liver Foie Gras.
30 stalks of green asparagus.
Water (to cook asparagus).
4-6 white mushrooms.
1 lemon (juice only).
1 pint (600 ml)/2½ cups milk.
4 fl. oz (120 ml)/½ cup wine vinegar.
4 fl. oz (120 ml)/½ cup cream.
Salt & freshly ground black pepper.
Parsley to garnish.

Clean and peel asparagus. Cut in half and cook heads and stalks separately. The stalks first as they take 4-6 minutes in boiling water with a pinch of salt, (heads, 2-4 minutes). Wash and slice mushrooms, sprinkle with lemon juice. Place the milk in a stainless steel saucepan, add mushrooms and cook gently for 10 minutes. Strain and place milk in a blender with the asparagus stalks and vinegar. Blend with cream to obtain a thick sauce. Season to taste. Cut foie gras in 12 slices. Cook without oil or grease in a non-stick pan for 1 minute on each side over a high flame until slightly golden. Remove and drain on absorbent kitchen paper. Spread sauce on serving dish. Place the foie gras slices on sauce and decorate with mushrooms, asparagus heads and parsley. Serve immediately,

Boiled Leg of Lamb with Caper Sauce.

3 lb (1.35 kilo) leg of lamb.
Bechamel Sauce with capers and small pieces of butter.

Weigh the lamb exactly and place in a pan just large enough to hold it. Just cover the meat with a mild chicken or beef stock. The stock must be weak so as not to destroy the taste of the meat. If too strong, dilute with water. Remove the joint and heat stock to boiling. Return the meat to pan and simmer for a further 15 minutes per lb, not one minute more. Serve with a light Bechamel Sauce to which capers have been added. Add enough butter (in small pieces) to suit your taste.

Irish Blackcurrant Cream.

11 oz (310 grams) strawberries.
11 oz (310 grams) wild strawberries.
11 oz (310 grams) redcurrants.
11 oz (310 grams) blackcurrants.
2 leaves gelatine.
17 fl. oz (½ litre)/2 cups water.
9 oz (250 grams)/1 cup castor sugar.
Egg custard. Whipped cream.

Clean, top and tail the fruit. Cut strawberries into two or four pieces depending on the size. Divide strawberries and redcurrants equally among 6 sundae glasses. Put gelatine to steep in small quantity of cold water. Liquidize blackcurrants in blender. Heat the water and sugar gently for 10 minutes, when boiling add blackcurrants and gelatine. Pour mixture over strawberries and allow to set. Make an egg custard, when cold, mix with whipped cream and serve with the fruit.

The Park Hotel Kenmare

T he Park Hotel Kenmare, built as a hotel has been successfully transformed into the elegance of a stately home. It has been filled with sumptuous works of art, Flemish tapestries and antiques. Notable is the 17th century Napolitan water cistern painted with Venus arising out of the sea, hoisted on guilded dolphins. Nearby are the torch-bearing "Peace and Plenty" (illustrated).

The hotel was opened as one of the Great Southern Railway Hotels in 1897 and sold in 1980. It was restored at enormous cost. Outside it still retains its solid castle-like Victorian facade sitting in eleven acres of manicured garden. Inside the old railway hotel is now a place of baronial elegance. It has fifty bedrooms and six luxurious suites all with marble bathrooms. The pride of the hotel is its food. Service, presentation and taste are quite exceptional as is the setting. Added to all this you are in the middle of some of the lovliest countryside in Ireland.

The Park Hotel,
Kenmare,
Co. Kerry,

The architect of The Park Hotel was James Franklin Fuller who built Kylemore, Ashford Castle, Mt Falcon Castle and Tinakilly House.

Avocado in Puff Pastry with a Fresh Tomato Sauce.

1 large ripe avocado.
2 oz (55 grams) crabmeat.
8 oz (225 grams) puff pastry.

Tomato Sauce.

1 lb 3 ½ oz (550 grams) ripe tomatoes, (skinned and seeded).
1 ½ oz (45 grams) shallots/spring onions.
½ clove garlic.
2 sprigs thyme and rosemary.
2 fl. oz (60 ml)/ ¼ cup chicken stock, (1 stock cube)
Salt and freshly ground black pepper.

Make sure all the seeds, skin and excessive juice have been removed from the tomatoes. Sauté shallots and garlic in a non-stick pan for 3-4 minutes, stirring constantly. Add herbs and sauté for about 1 minute. Add tomatoes and stock, simmer for 10-12 minutes. Remove herbs and purée the rest in a blender. Place sauce back in pan, bring to the boil, skim and season to taste.

Halve avocado, remove nut and skin. Sprinkle with lemon juice and season. Check crabmeat for shell. Squeeze out excessive liquid and season to taste. Fill half avocado hollow with crabmeat. Roll pastry to 5" x 4" (12.5 x 10 cm), less than ⅛ inch (4 mm) thick. Place over avocado and fold under, egg wash and put on an oiled tray. Bake at 400°F/200°C/Reg 6 for 5-7 minutes. Put sauce on plate, place avocado on hollow side down and garnish.

Ribbons of Wild Duckbreast with Two Sauces.

2 plump young birds.
2 tblspns oil.
Salt & pepper.

Juniper Berry Sauce.

6 Juniper Berries.
½ pint (300 ml)/1 ¼ cups wild duck stock.
1 glass of 'Old' port.
1 glass of red wine.
½ tspn of thyme.
Little cream & unsalted butter.
Seasoning.

Pinekernel Sauce.

2 oz (55 grams) pinekernels.
Squeeze of lemon juice.
1 glass dry white wine.
4 chopped shallots/spring onions.
Hint of mace.
½ pint (300 ml)/1 ¼ cups cream.
Salt & pepper.

Prepare the ducks for roasting. Place in a roasting tray and sprinkle a little oil over them. Season with salt and freshly ground pepper. Roast until flesh is firm, but still pink. Allow to rest in a cool place for about one hour. Remove the breasts from the two birds. Skin them and carve into six or eight thin slices depending on the size of the duckbreasts.

Juniper Berry Sauce.

Put the wine, port, juniper berries and thyme in a heavy saucepan and allow to reduce almost completely. Add the wild duck stock and allow to reduce further until the sauce is of the required consistency. Strain through a sieve. Whisk in a little diced unsalted butter over a gentle heat. Season with salt and pepper. Add a couple of tblspns of cream.

Pinekernel Sauce.

Finely chop the pinekernels. Sweat the chopped shallots. Add the mace and coriander, a squeeze of lemon juice, then the cream and pinekernels. Simmer gently for 4-5 minutes until the flavour from the pinekernels has been infused into the sauce. Strain again, reheat and correct the seasoning.

Serving.

Take four large heated plates. Coat the plates with a little of each sauce. Arrange the carved duckbreasts in a fan shape. Garnish each plate with a small fennel frond and a poached ring of red pepper. Heat through for a few minutes in the oven and serve.

Apple Pie du 'Parc'.

Pastry.

1 lb (450 grams)/3 ½ cups flour.
10 oz (285 grams)/1 ¼ cups butter.
4 oz (110 grams)/½ cup sugar.
2 eggs (whole).
Pinch salt.

Filling.

4-6 large cooking apples.
½ pint (300 ml)/1 ¼ cups sugar syrup.
½ tblspn sultanas.
Juice of ½ lemon.
½ tspn cinnamon.

Syrup.

½ pint (300 mls)/1 ¼ cups water.
4 oz (110 grams)/½ cup sugar.

Bring to the boil and add the juice of ½ lemon.

Pastry.

Rub together the flour, butter and salt. Add sugar and beaten eggs and bind together. Chill overnight.

Filling.

Peel and slice apples (thinly) and place into hot syrup, leave until syrup has cooled, remove and mix in sultanas and cinnamon. Cool completely.

To assemble.

Grease well a 10 inch (25 centimetre) flan ring and base. Roll out pastry to desired thickness and line mould. Trim edges. Place filling into pastry until just below level of rim. Roll out remaining pastry. Place on top. Seal edges by pressing between finger and thumb. Chill in refrigerator. Beat together 1 egg and 2 tblspns of milk, and brush lightly onto pie and bake at 380°F/190°C/Reg 5-6 for ½-¾ hour or until golden brown. Serve hot or cold with lightly whipped cream or with hot fresh egg custard.

Mid Victorian villa dramatically situated overlooking Caragh Lake and the Macgillycuddy Reeks. The architect was William Atkins of Co. Cork. Vegetable garden was laid out by Col. Ferrard and head gardener John Murphy around 1935. The rest of the garden was planted with many rare trees and shrubs by German couple, Dr. and Mrs Schaper who added the very tasteful extension to the house. Now owned by their daughter and son-in-law Ines and Michael Braasch. Ines spent much of her childhood at Caragh Lodge. Overall winners of 1982 National Garden award.

36

Caragh Lodge

C aragh Lodge is a lovely old house of indeterminate age and history situated near Killarney in a park sweeping down to the shores of Caragh Lake with the lofty Macgillycuddy Reeks beyond. The bedrooms are most cunningly converted stables or garden cottages. They are spacious, sunny and welcoming and each one leads out into the park with paths leading to the lake shore. I stayed at Caragh Lodge in superb spring weather in early May when the magnolias, rhododendrons, lilacs and azaleas were in full bloom– a magnificent riot of colour. The main house itself has retained its original country house character, with cornice mouldings and marble fire places. Many old prints and paintings decorate the walls. Every window views the superb garden, lake and mountains. The dining room, dominated by a large chandelier, is roomy and comfortable. Cuisine leans towards the continental but with Irish bread and home grown fruit and vegetables. The wine list is very impressive. Both Ines and Michael Braasch trained in hotel management in Germany and as one would expect from not one, but two trained managers working in harmony, everything is expertly run!

Caragh Lodge,
Caragh Lake,
Co. Kerry.

Crab Cakes.

2lb (900 grams) crabmeat.
7 slices white bread (crusts removed) diced.
¼ green pepper, chopped.
1 ½ tblspns parsley, chopped.
2 eggs.
10 tblspns mayonnaise.
½ tspn dry mustard.
½ tspn salt.
3 shakes tabasco.
3 shakes Worcestershire sauce.
1 tblspn lemon juice.

Beat eggs lightly and add mayonnaise, mustard, salt, tabasco, worcestershire sauce and lemon juice. In another bowl lightly mix crabmeat, bread pieces, green pepper and parsley. Carfully fold in the egg mixture, being careful not to break the crabmeat pieces. Form into cakes and pan fry in butter. Serve immediately. Yield 8-10 cakes.

Note. This can also be used to stuff fish, giant king prawns or to bake in ramekins.

Kalbshaxe–Veal Haxe on mirepoix.

1 veal haxe, (hock or knuckles).
Salt and pepper.
Mirepoix, (mixed, chopped carrots, onions, celery root, and leeks).
Bayleaf.
1 sprig thyme.
Peppercorns.
Onions.
Carrots.
Potatoes.
½ lb (225 grams) piece smoked, cooked bacon (lean).

Season the veal haxe. Lay the mirepoix on foil with the haxe on top, add the bay leaf and thyme. Wrap it up in the foil and bake in a hot oven for 1½-2 hours. Just before the haxe is cooked, open the foil, baste the meat with the juices, and let brown on top.

To go beside the haxe when serving:

Peel very small onions (spring onions are best) and glaze them in butter with a little sugar until they are brown, leave to simmer in some jus. Cook carrot and potato pieces, strain and add a little knob of butter. Blanche the bacon, cut into pieces and add to the onion, carrot and potato pieces. This is served with the haxe. Serve with dauphine potatoes and whatever vegetables are in season.

Rum Crème.

3 leaves of gelatine.
4 egg yolks.
2½ oz sugar (65 grams)/¼ cup sugar.
2 drops of vanilla essence.
6 tblspns of rum, (brown rum).
4 fl. oz (120 ml)/½ cup cream.
2 oz (55 grams) flake chocolate.
Rind of ½ lemon.

Soak the leaf gelatine in a little cold water. Whisk the egg yolks, sugar and vanilla essence. Add salt, lemon rind and rum. Heat the wet gelatine over low heat until dissolved. Stir into the egg mixture and leave in the fridge to set for approx. 10 minutes. Whip the cream and fold carefully into the rum mixture. Put into a serving dish or individual dishes and leave in the fridge to set. Just before serving decorate with flaked chocolate.

Assolas

The history of 'Assolas' from 1674-1714 is lost in the mists of time: however, in 1714 it became the property of Rev. Francis Gore who enlarged the estate. Rev. Gore, a man of means and influence, was the rector of Castlemanger Church. In those days a previous road (still visible today) forded the river beside Assolas House, and legend tells us that Rev. Gore always hung a lantern high on the walls of the house: a welcome light to guide travellers on their way. It is reported that he saved many lives from swollen rivers and from bands of highway men roaming the area. Assolas was always open to receive the wounded, and so well known became his warm and friendly light, that the ford became known in Gaelic as 'Ata Solas' (Ford of Light). The Anglicised version has become abbreviated to 'Assolas'. Rev. Gore was a just and humane man when men in his position were feared and disliked. To this day, in Castlemanger Church a private pew is reserved for the residents of Assolas as a tribute to Rev. Gore. It is generally accepted that prior to the suppression of the Catholic church by Queen Elizabeth I, Assolas was occupied by a community of Catholic monks. The present stone outhouses, with still-visible castings of closed-up windows, remind us of its monastic past. Of interest is the 'Lepers Peep' still clearly visible.

Many ancient Yew trees in the grounds were planted, in another non-atomic age, to supply good quality bows to our bow and arrow ancestors.

The house is difficult to locate but ask, ask and ask again, no-one minds in Ireland. When you get there you are warmly welcomed by the Bourke family. The guests are a very cosmopolitan group, a great air of hospitality prevails and there is food galore of a very high standard.

Assolas Country House,
Kanturk,
Co. Cork.

The original house, the centre of the present residence, seems to date from the early 1600's. The shape of the windows, with their very old hand blown glass with all its imperfections; the exterior rough stone and mortar strengthened by the addition of horse hair and ox blood; the walls, of great depth, four and a half foot thick, are all in character. The eastern wing with beautifully rounded frontage would appear to have been added a century later. The large old flagstone kitchen on the ground floor was in everyday use until 1915. Unfortunately no records are available to tell us when the front wing was built.

41

Tarragon Cream Dressing for Avocado Salad.
Dressing
2 eggs.
4 rounded tblspns of castor sugar.
6 tblspns tarragon vinegar.
Salt & pepper.
½ pint (300 ml)/1¼ cups double cream.

Beat the egg and add sugar. Gradually add vinegar beating all the time. Stand the bowl in a pan of boiling water. beating until it begins to thicken. Set aside. Partially whip cream and fold into mixture when cold. Halve and stone the avocados, serve on a bed of lettuce and cover with the dressing.

This dressing keeps well under refrigeration if cream is omitted. Can also be used to dress individual salads such as broccoli and bacon.

Fillet of Salmon Mousseline.

Prepare a Hollandaise Sauce, adding fine zest of lemon, butter and cream.

Hollandaise Sauce.

1 tblspn white wine vinegar.
2 large egg yolks.
4-5 oz (110-140 grams)/½ cup butter.
Lemon zest.

Using a double-boiler, heat water until hot but not boiling. In the pan or bowl which is to go over the water, whisk the vinegar and egg yolks. Place over the hot water. Stirring all the time, add the butter piece by piece. Let each piece melt before adding the next. If the sauce shows any sign of curdling or thickening too quickly, remove from heat immediately. It should be smooth and fairly thick. To make the Mousseline Sauce, take lightly whipped cream and fold in 1/3 as much as Hollandaise. Keep warm in a double boiler–use as quickly as possible. Take fillet of salmon and season with salt, pepper and lemon balm, (no lemon juice, as this softens the flesh). Wrap in lightly buttered foil and bake in the oven. Remove from foil, then–remove skin and serve with freshly made mousseline sauce. Garnish with cress. Serve *immediately* with new potatoes in parsley butter and garden mange-tout. *Mange-tout,* a pea of which the pod is eaten as well as the seed. Mousseline can be given various herb flavours by adding chopped herbs whilst making the Hollandaise Sauce.

Fluffy Almond Tart.

1lb (450 grams) of shortcrust pastry.
8 oz (225 grams) of cream cheese.
4 eggs (separated).
3 fl. oz. (90 mls)/1/3 cup of cream.
2 tspns grated orange rind.
½ tspn almond essence.
3 tblspns sugar.
Split almonds to finish.

Line a flan ring with pastry and bake blind for 10 minutes at 350°F/180°C/ Regulo 4. Beat together all remaining ingredients *except* egg whites. Whip whites until soft and fold into mixture. Pour into baked pastry case. Sprinkle with split almonds. Return to oven and bake for a further 25-30 minutes. Serve fresh from oven.

To bake blind; Place the pastry in the flan ring without stretching it. Put greaseproof paper or lightly greased foil on top of this. To prevent pastry from rising put rice or other dried beans on top.

43

Longueville. Original house was built in 1720 and retained as a centre piece when two wings were added in 1800. The exotic conservatory was added in 1866. The Regency plasterwork ceiling is by an Italian artist.

Longueville House and Presidents' Restaurant.

I n this grand old house, built over two centuries ago and situated in a 500 acre wooded estate, you are surrounded by many of Ireland's beauty spots. The twenty guest bedrooms are all individually decorated in superb period style. The public rooms, too, are very elegant but with warmth and comfort. The restaurant is fully licensed, and the food recommended by many international food guides. Ireland's only vineyard is located on the farm.

The history of Longueville reflects the history of Ireland itself. The lands originally owned by Donough O'Callaghan who fought with Catholic Confederates after the collapse of the 1641 Rebellion, were forfeited to Cromwell. The house was built by the Longfield family who appear to have acquired the property from Purdon, a soldier of Cromwell.

Richard Longfield was created Baron Longueville in 1795 and changed the name of the house to Longueville. William O'Callaghan, whose ancestors were deprived of their land by Cromwell, repurchased it in 1938 and it is now owned and run by Michael and Jane O'Callaghan, and their son William.

From the house there is a wonderful view of The Blackwater river and the ruined Dromineen Castle, ancient seat of long past O'Callaghan's.

Longueville House,
Mallow,
Co. Cork.

Game terrine with Goosberry Chutney.

1 lb (450 grams) minced pork.
2 quail, boned, rolled and browned.
2 oz (55 grams) finely chopped onions.
1 clove garlic, crushed.
1 cooking apple, chopped.
1 tspn fresh herbs, (e.g. parsley, sage, chives, thyme).
Salt and pepper.
2 oz (55 grams) hazelnuts.
1 egg.
¼ bottle cider.

Combine all ingredients together and put into a covered terrine. Place in a bain-marie and cook in a very low oven (200°F/90°C/Reg ⅛) for 2-2½ hours. Test, press and leave to cool.

Gooseberry Chutney.

4 lb (1.8 kg) gooseberries.
4 onions.
1 oz (30 grams)/1½ tblspns salt.
1½ lb 675 grams)/3 cups brown sugar.
½ lb (225 grams)/1½ cups sultanas.
2 pints (1.2 litres)/5 cups vinegar.
1 tspn dry mustard.
¼ tspn cayenne pepper,

Top and tail the gooseberries. Chop the onions and put into a greased saucepan with all the other ingredients. Stir over a low heat until sugar has completely dissolved. Bring up to the boil, then reduce heat and simmer until thick and pulpy, stirring frequently. Pour into sterilized pots and close tightly.

Fillets of Black Sole Rosas.

12 medium fillets of black sole.
24 cooked prawns.
12 blanched spinach or sorrel leaves.
White wine sauce to serve.

Fish Cream.

½ lb (225 grams) trimmings of black sole, prawns or scallops,
3 times ratio cream to fish, (approx. 1¼ pint/725 ml).
1 egg white.

Gunge up fish trimmings, prawns or scallops in a food processor with the egg white and sieve into a bowl which is over ice (this prevents the mixture cracking)–gradually beat in the cream and season.

Batten out the fish fillets. Spread on a tspn of fish cream with a spatula. Blanch the spinach or sorrel leaf and wrap a cooked prawn in it. Place this on the fish cream and add another little bit of cream on top–then fold over the fillet.

Cook for 3-4 minutes in a steamer. Serve with a white wine sauce and decorate with remaining prawns and chervil.

White Wine Sauce.

Reduce ½ bottle of medium dry wine with sliced shallots to about one third of a glass, and then add 1 pint/600ml/2½ cups cream and reduce again to half. Finish by beating in approx 4oz/110 grams/½ cup unsalted butter (away from the direct heat) and finish with a dash of lemon juice and season to taste. Strain.

To serve:

Put the sauce on the plate first and then place the two fillets at an angle and decorate with chervil and cooked prawns.

Vanilla Ice-Cream with Fresh Fruit in Season.

3 egg yolks.
4 oz (110 grams)/½ cup castor sugar.
½ pint (300 ml) 1½ cups cream.
Few drops vanilla essence.

Beat the egg-yolks and sugar together until very creamy. In another bowl, whip the cream until thick. Add the vanilla essence to the yolks and lightly fold in the cream. Transfer to a large plastic container, cover with a lid and freeze until firm.

N.B. Any purée of fresh fruit and sugar can be added to the above to make a flavoured ice-cream. (You will need about ¼ pint (150 mls) good, thick purée, sweetened to taste, for the above quantity).

The original Tower House belonged to the O'Loughlins, Princes of Burren who intermarried with the Protestant Martyns of Galway in 1632 and so preserved their Estates. The 18th century house was extended in 1880, restored and made into an hotel in 1965. The original stove and arched fireplace of the kitchen survive in the lounge with the chair of Edward Martyn recently acquired by the present owners.

Gregans Castle Hotel

Gregans Castle Hotel is a good centre for touring the Burren. The Burren occupies about 100 square miles of Co. Clare. Geologists call it 'karst' after similar regions in Yugoslavia. The area is of outstanding interest to geologists and botanists. The entire region has a complex system of underground lakes and turloughs (lakes which disappear overnight) and streams which disappear into pot holes. There is much evidence of prehistoric occupation with numerous dolmans and forts. Visually it presents as a lunar like landscape with its own distinctive flora.

Gregans Castle Hotel,
Nr Ballyvaughan,
Co. Clare.

Home Smoked Sausages.

12 of your favourite pork sausages.
2 bacon rashers.
Garlic.
Green Salad
Oil (preferably olive).
Vinegar.
Seasoning.

Pierce each sausage in about four places and insert a sliver of garlic and a tiny piece of bacon rasher. Using one of those simple fisherman's smokers, (available in most sports goods shops), smoke the sausages for about half an hour. Leave to cool in the smoker. When cool, cut each sausage into small pieces about ½ inch (1.5 cm) long. Make a green salad of available items such as lettuce, green peppers, thin cucumber slices, and endives. Make a salad dressing using two parts oil to one part vinegar. Add seasoning to taste, and toss together the salad, sausage pieces and dressing. Serve slightly chilled.

Brochette of Fruit and Chicken with Avocado Sauce.

6 chicken breasts, skinned and boned.
Juice of one large lemon.
Juice of one orange.
6 tblspns white wine (dry).
1 tspn basil.
1 tspn thyme.
Ground black pepper.
2 green or red peppers cut into chunks.
3 small onions cut into quarters.
12 prunes (soaked overnight).
2 firm bananas.
12 rashers streaky bacon.

Avocado Sauce.

2 ripe avocados.
Juice of 1 lemon.
8 fl. oz (250 ml)/1 cup natural yoghurt.
Chopped chives.
Chopped parsley.
Seasoning.

In a bowl, place the lemon juice, white wine, seasoning and herbs. Into this marinade place the chicken breasts, (cut up into good size cubes) and leave for 1-2 hours. Meanwhile, cut the peppers into chunks, the onions into quarters, and the bananas into strips about 2 inches (5 cm) long. Remove the stones from the prunes. Stretch each rasher using the back of a knife, and make sure the rind has been removed. Wrap a piece of the stretched rasher around each prune and each slice of banana. With an eye to appearance, carefully arrange all these ingredients including the chicken onto 6 skewers. Brush with the marinade juices and grill most carefully for about 15 minutes until you are satisfied that the chicken is cooked through. Do not over brown or burn. Meanwhile make the sauce. Mix together the flesh of the ripe avocados and other ingredients. An electric blender is best for this, although it can be done by hand with a fork. With the sauce in a jug, warm gently by placing jug into a saucepan of hot water and stirring. Spread the sauce thinly yet consistently over a warm plate, and place the brochette of fruit and chicken in the centre. Carefully withdraw the skewer before serving.

Oranges in Grand Marnier.

7 large oranges. (with as few pips as possible).
6 oz (170 grams)/¾ cup castor sugar.
6 tblspns Grand Marnier liqueur.

Peel the zest off one orange, and cut into very thin slices. Squeeze the juice from this orange and reserve. Cut all the pith and peel from remaining six oranges, and cut into thin slices. Arrange these slices overlapping in a bowl. Mix together the orange juice and Grand Marnier and pour over the oranges. Sprinkle over all the sugar. Chill well (preferably overnight). Just before serving, sprinkle with thin slices of zest.

Currarevagh House.

T he mansion sits in a 150 acre lake-side demesne on the shores of Lough Corrib. The lake, I am told, has 365 islands. If you feel like checking the number, it could be a unique holiday experience. The trim little 19th century boathouse is your "open sesame". After a robust Irish breakfast you can tour Connemara and the Burren, then bring your appetite back with you to enjoy a meal of traditional food based on local produce.

Currarevagh House,
Oughterard,
Connemara,
Co. Galway.

The house was built by the Hodgson family, ancestors of the present occupants. Built in 1847 it replaced an earlier one. Conceived on a grand scale in the Italian manner, it has the air of a London Club magically wafted on to a wooded promatory, to overlook the forests and islands of Lough Corrib. The windows are early examples of plate glass, the fireplaces are robustly Victorian.

Terrine of Smoked Salmon.

6 small slices of smoked salmon.
8 oz (225 grams) flaked smoked salmon.
2 level dessertspns of powdered gelatine mixed with ½ pint (300 ml)/1¼ cups warm water.
2 egg yolks.
1 heaped tspn Dijon mustard.
1 heaped tspn tomato purée.
Juice of 2 lemons.
6 fl. oz (170 ml)/¾ cup nut oil.
8 fl. oz (250 ml)/1 cup milk.
2 oz (55 grams)/¼ cup cream.
Plenty of salt and black pepper.

Dissolve the gelatine in the water over a gentle heat and leave to cool. Dip slices of smoked salmon into the gelatine and line the bottom of six ramekin dishes. Put yolks, lemon juice, mustard, tomato purée, oil, salt and pepper into a liquidizer and combine. Put this mixture into a jug and add the gelatine. Put flaked smoked salmon, milk and cream into the liquidiser and combine. Add this mixture to the above and pour into ramekin dishes. Leave to set for 4-6 hours and turn out.
Serve with herbs.

Baked Stuffed Leg of Veal with Lemon Sauce.

6 lb (2.7 kg) boned leg of veal.
2 oz (55 grams)/¼ cup margarine.
1 onion.
4 oz (110 grams)/1 cup breadcrumbs.
Thyme and sage.
Grated peel of 1 lemon.
Salt & pepper.

Remove as much fat as is possible from the veal and leave flat. Combine all the other ingredients and make the stuffing. Spread over the veal and roll, secure with string. Put the veal into a large baking dish in which there is one inch of water. Spread a liberal amount of margarine over the veal and cover with foil. Bake in a hot oven for 20 minutes and then reduce to 350°F/180°C/Regulo 4 for ¾ hour. Remove foil, brown in a hot oven for 10 minutes and then slice it when hot.

Lemon Sauce.

1 onion.
2 oz (55 grams)/¼ cup margarine.
2 oz (55 grams)/scant ½ cup flour.
½ pint (300 ml)/1¼ cups chicken stock.
2 egg yolks.
3 oz (85 grams)/⅜ cup cream.
Salt & pepper.
Juice of 2 lemons.

Melt margarine, add the diced onion and cook until soft. Add flour and make a roux. Gradually add the chicken stock and cook for five minutes. Strain and leave to cool. Make a liaison with the yolks and cream and add to the above mixture. Add the lemon juice, season to taste and serve hot with the veal.

Chocolate Praline Pudding.

3 oz (85 grams) plain chocolate.
1 pkt of sponge fingers.
1 tblspn Tia Maria.
1 tblspn brandy.
1 tblspn cold strong coffee.
1 tblspn milk.
¾ pint (450 ml)/1¾ cups cream.
1 tblspn castor sugar.
6 oz (170 grams)/1½ cups coarse praline.

Melt the chocolate and leave to cool. Mix the Tia Maria, brandy, coffee and milk. Dip half the sponge fingers into it and line the bottom of a long tin with them. Whip the cream and add the castor sugar and cooled chocolate. Spread half over the biscuits, add half the praline then the rest of the biscuits dipped in the coffee solution. Put most of the remaining praline on top of the biscuits. If there is any of the coffee solution left over, combine it with the remaining cream and spread over the praline. Leave in the freezer for 2-3 hours. Turn out and sprinkle with praline.

Cashel House

A feature of Cashel House is the award winning 50 acre garden, with rhodedendrons, azaleas, camelias and beautiful rare magnolias. Situated at the head of Cashel Bay with its own little beach, the house has the Atlantic Ocean almost on its doorstep. Inside it is warm and comfortable with turf fires and fresh flowers everywhere. The bedrooms are excellent, attractively furnished with character and charm. I found the food and wine very good. A word of warning– there are two Cashels on the map of Ireland– don't turn up at the other one and ask for the Atlantic Ocean!

Cashel House Hotel,
Cashel,
Co. Galway.

*Cashel House, built in 1850 for Captain Hazel by Geoffrey Emmerson who is said to have designed it.
Kay McEvilly, his great-grand daughter with her husband Dermot are the present owners.*

Seafood Pâté.

4 oz (110 grams) smoked salmon.
4 oz (110 grams) smoked mackerel, skinned.
5 oz (140 grams) seafood (scallops, lobster pieces etc.).
12-16 oz (340-450 grams)/1½-2 cups soft butter.
Salt & pepper.
Chopped chives.
Lemon juice.
Spinach leaves (cooked).

1st layer.
Blend smoked salmon and lemon juice. Add the butter (7 oz/200 grams/⅞ cup) in small bits very carefully so that the butter does not curdle.

2nd layer.
Blend smoked mackerel and lemon juice. Add the butter (4 oz/110 grams/½ cup) in small bits. Blend carefully until of smooth consistency.

3rd layer.
Blend scallops, lobster, and lemon juice. Add the butter. (5 oz/140 grams/⅝ cup) and salt, pepper and chives. Line a pâté dish with greaseproof paper. Separate each pâté with spinach leaves and chill.

Chicken with Orange and Mustard Sauce.

3.5 lb (1.6 kg chicken).
Dijon mustard.
Brown sugar.
Orange juice.
1 pint (600 ml)/2½ cups cream.
Salt & pepper.

Cover the chicken with mustard and a little brown sugar and orange juice. Cook, basteing often. Set chicken aside. Keep warm. To make the sauce, heat the juices in the pan and add the cream. Cook for 10 minutes to thicken, add salt and pepper. Serve with chicken.

Yoghurt Mousse, with Pineapple, Strawberries or Kiwi Fruit and a Caramel Sauce.

2½ fl. oz (75 ml) milk.
4 egg yolks.
1 oz (30 grams)/2 tblspns sugar.
6 leaves gelatine.
¾ pint (450 ml)/1⅞ cups yoghurt.
Juice of 1 lemon.
½ pint (300 ml)/1¼ cups cream.
4 egg whites.

Sauce.

7 oz (200 grams)/⅞ cup sugar.
Juice and zest of 2 oranges.
Juice of 1 lemon.
3 oz (85 grams)/⅜ cup apricot purée.
2-3 fl. oz/(60-85 ml) Crème de Cacao or Curaçao.
1 fresh or tinned pineapple.
OR 8 oz (225 grams) fresh or frozen strawberries.
OR 2 kiwi fruits sliced.

To prepare the mousse, bring the milk to the boil. Cream the egg yolks and sugar well; gradually add the boiled milk and mix well. Return to the heat stirring constantly until the mixture starts to thicken, but do not boil. Soak the gelatine in a little cold water, then stir into the hot mixture. Add the yoghurt and lemon juice. Whisk until smooth. Leave to cool. Whip the egg whites and fold in the sugar. When the yoghurt mixture is cold fold in the cream (whipped) and egg whites. Pour the mixture into individual dishes and place in the fridge to set.

To make the sauce: melt the sugar over heat until it becomes a slightly dark caramel. Add the juice and zest of the oranges, lemon and apricot purée. Mix well and add the crème de cacao and recook the sauce slightly. Wash and cut fruit and arrange on the set mousse and coat with the sauce, just before serving.

59

A regency villa of the 1820's. The gardens were extended by Edward and Liz O'Brien who bought it in 1950 from the Land Commission and sold it to Paddy and Anne Foyle in 1971. A wing was added by architect Leo Mansfield. The house has spectacular views of Ballinakill Bay, the Twelve Pins and Kylemore.

Rosleague Manor

If you enjoy being a guest in a period house, you couldn't do better than stay at Rosleague, a Regency manor house commanding a superb position on the Atlantic Coast of Connemara. Furnished with well chosen antiques it has been turned into a place of infinite charm by brother and sister team Anne and Paddy Foyle. Guests have included many of the world's rich and famous. The food has won prestigious awards internationally and the Irish Tourist Board's award of excellence.

Rosleague Manor,
Letterfrack,
Co. Galway.

Rosleagues's most requested recipe: Mulligatawny Soup.

1 heaped tblspn hot curry powder.
1 heaped tblspn tomato purée.
1 small onion–diced.
1 small cooking apple–cored and diced.
½ cup uncooked rice.
2½ pints/1.4 litres/6¼ cups good chicken stock.
At least 1 tblspn lime juice.

Fry the onion in a little oil until soft, *not* brown, stir in the curry powder, tomato purée and rice. Stir quickly and let the whole lot come to the boil. Add the diced apple and when the rice is completely soft put the mixture through a blender or mouli. The soup must be really smooth and 'silky' in texture. Return to the pan and add the lime juice cordial to taste or, if you prefer, a little pineapple juice. At this stage a little cream wouldn't go astray. Heat gently again but do not boil. If the mixture gets too thick, thin it down with a little chicken stock. Garnish with a swirl of cream and a sprinkling of paprika.

Stuffed Turkey Breton-Style.

Stuffing:
Some white or brown, stale breadcrumbs (approx. 3 cups).
1 lb (450 grams) pork sausages.
5 oz/150 grams/1 cup raisins.
20 soaked and stoned prunes.
2½ oz/70 grams/½ cup chopped almonds–flaked or chopped, (optional but nice!).
Large glass of port (or cooking sherry can be substituted).
All the giblets especially the liver finely chopped–omit the neck of course!
Some thyme and lovage and any other desired herbs.
2 chopped onions and a little garlic.

Fry the onions and garlic in lots of butter until soft, *not* brown. Add other ingredients and, depending on consistency, add or omit more breadcrumbs. The mixture should hold its shape but not be too dry– use your judgement. Stuff and roast turkey in the normal way.

Simple Almond and Walnut Cake (top secret recipe).

10 oz (280 grams)/2 cups white flour.
8 oz (225 grams)/1 cup castor sugar.
2-3 level tspns baking powder.
6 fl. oz (175 ml)/¾ cup milk.
4 oz (110 grams)/½ cup softened butter and vegetable shortening mixed.
2 eggs.
1 tspn almond essence.
2 oz (55 grams)/½ cup finely chopped walnuts (or 1 small packet).

Measure everything except nuts into a large mixing bowl. Blend at low speed until mixed (about 3 minutes) then at high speed. Finally fold in the chopped nuts and pour into two loaf tins. Bake for 50-60 minutes 350°F/180°C/Regulo 4-5.

Newport House

A stately ivy covered mansion rich in history and handsomely decorated with period furniture. It has elegance and atmosphere. Bedrooms are of country house size. The food comes mainly from the garden and farm, the fish from the private fishery and the salmon is home smoked. The splendid meal I remember with pleasure. If fishing is your "thing", it would be hard to find a more idyllic place.

Newport House,
Newport,
Co. Mayo.

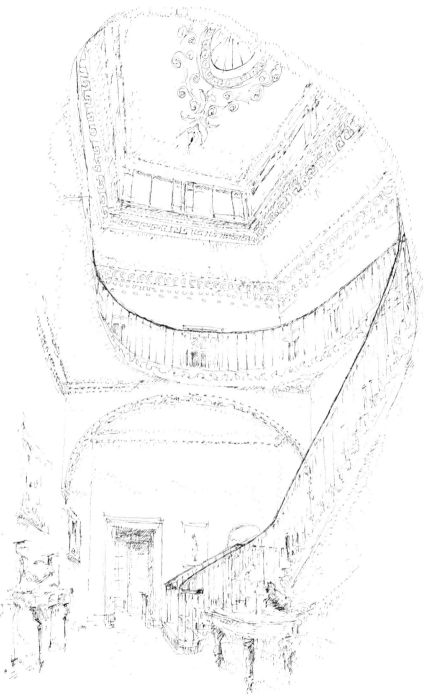

Newport House was once the seat of the O'Donnells, one of the "Wild Geese" families, Counts of the Holy Roman Empire. It is sited overlooking the Newport River. Its origin is the mid 18th century. The entrance hall leads into a small domed lobby that very dramatically opens up to a regency arched and galleried staircase hall lit by a central lantern and eliptical dome. Recent restoration and decoration was completed in 1987 by owners Mr & Mrs Kieran Thompson.

Fresh Prawns en-croûte with Provençale Sauce.

8 oz (225 grams) puff pastry.
1 lb (450 grams) fresh prawn tails.
2 oz (55 grams)/¼ cup garlic butter.
1 egg.

Roll out puff pastry in a rectangular shape ⅛ inch (3 mm) thick. Set aside for 20 minutes. Cut out four 1½ inch (4 cm) square pieces. Place freshly peeled prawns of equal quantity on the centre of each square. Put ½ oz (15 grams)/1 tblspn of garlic butter on top prawns. Brush the four corners with beaten up egg. Fold opposite four corners to meet in centre and brush with the remainder of egg. Gently place the pastry case on a floured baking sheet and leave in a cool place for approximately one hour.

Provençale Sauce.

1 lb (450 grams) tomatoes, (5 large).
1 small onion, (finely chopped).
2 oz (55 grams)/¼ cup garlic butter.
Pinch of fresh thyme.

Melt the 2 oz (55 grams)/½ cup of garlic butter add the finely chopped onion and thyme. Cook without colour. Add the blanched diced tomatoes. Cook slowly for ten minutes. Season with salt and pepper.

To Serve:
Cook the pastry cases in a hot oven 400°F/200°C/Reg 6 for about 15 minutes. When cooked, place a generous spoonful of provençale sauce on the plate. Place the pastry case in the middle.

Parslied Chicken Guerard.

1 Chicken, 3.5 lb. (1,575 kilos).

Stuffing 1.
¾ oz (20 grams)/1½ tblspns butter.
1 tblspn parsley.
1 tblspn water.
1½ tspns salt.
1½ tspns pepper.
2 oz (55 grams)/¼ cup natural yoghurt.
Juice of 1 lemon.

Stuffing 2.
3 tblspns parsley, (chopped).
1 tblspn chives.
1 tspn tarragon.
2 tblspns shallots.
2 oz (55 grams)/½ cup mushrooms.
2 oz (55 grams)/2 rashers streaky bacon.

Sauce.
¾ oz 20 grams)/1½ tblspns butter.
1 lb (450 grams) chopped shallots.
1 tblspn sherry vinegar.
1/3 pint (200 ml) stock.
4 tblspns cream.
1 oz (30 grams)/2 tblspns softened butter.
¾ oz (20 grams) tomato pulp, (no skin).
1 tblspn chervil.

Blend together all ingredients in part 1. Put the butter mixture (1) in a large bowl. Mix in the finely chopped herbs, shallots, mushrooms, bacon and beat together with a fork to obtain a smooth stuffing.

Stuffing the chicken.

Lift the skin away from the breast and legs of the chicken (by sliding your fingers between the skin and flesh) working carefully and slowly to avoid tearing the skin. Insert the stuffing, again with your fingers patting it in an even layer over the breast and thighs.

Cooking the chicken.

Season the inside of the chicken with salt and pepper and roast (breast upwards) for 45 minutes (450°F/230°C/Reg 8) basting frequently. When the chicken is cooked, remove from oven. Transfer to dish and keep hot.

Preparing the sauce.

Remove fat from the roasting tin. Replace it with 1/3 oz (10 grams)/1 tblspn butter and add finely chopped shallots. Cook without colour, add the sherry vinegar, scraping up all the caramelised roasting juices. Reduce by ¾. Add chicken stock and cream. Reduce by 1/3. Finally beat in 1 oz (30 grams)/2 tblspns of butter in pieces. Strain the sauce through the wire sieve, add diced tomatoes and chervil. Keep hot in bain-marie.

Serving the chicken:

Cut the chicken into 8 pieces, leaving one piece of breast and thigh together. Arrange the pieces of chicken on serving dish and coat with hot sauce. Serve with buttered broccoli and boiled new potatoes.

Crème Brulée.

½ pint (300 ml)/1¼ cup cream.
3 eggs.
2 tblspns vanilla castor sugar
OR use unflavoured sugar and 1 tspn vanilla essence.

Empty cream & milk into a thick bottomed saucepan, bringing the creamy milk not quite to the boil. Lightly whisk the eggs with the sugar and vanilla. Add to the warmed creamy milk mixture. Make sure the cream mixture is not too hot (otherwise it will curdle). Half fill a roasting pan with boiling water to make a bain-marie and ladle the cream and egg mixture into small earthenware custard dishes. Stand the pudding in the pan and cook for 2-2½ hours at 250°F/120°C/Reg ½.

The pudding requires gentle cooking otherwise they will curdle. Test to see whether they have set by shaking gently. Cool overnight. The pudding must be cold before the brulée is added.

An hour before you serve the Crème Brulée, sprinkle brown sugar over each one and place under the grill until the sugar melts, spreads and browns. Watch over them to see the sugar does not burn. Serve with Langue-du-Chat finger biscuits.

Enniscoe House

The name 'Inniscoe' means 'Island of the Hound' and it is said to have originated from a family far back in Irish history, who were in possession of these lands and who were renowned breeders of greyhounds. The history of the house and estate revolves around the families and ancestors of the present occupants and is meticulously documented through family records of birth, marriages and deaths from 1163 to the present day.

Enniscoe is now a country house hotel with a comfortable aura–and with windows overlooking the peaceful parklands and distant lake, antique furniture and family portraits everywhere. My bedroom was of noble size complete with four poster bed. The home smoked trout with yoghurt sauce I had for dinner was excellent. If you plan to see Ireland, this is it– amid green fields and mountains. Even when it rains (and it does) it never pours– it's just soft Irish rain which keeps the "Emerald" in the landscape.

Enniscoe House,
Castlehill,
Nr Crossmolina,
Ballina,
Co. Mayo.

Enniscoe House, an early 18th century west of Ireland, four storied manor house, architecture attributed to John Roberts. Extended in 1790 and disguised to make a square double storied house on a grander scale. The new rooms encase the surprise of an elliptical staircase curving dizzily upwards beneath a glazed dome. Paintings are by the surrealist artist Mrs Nicholson who is mother of the owner.

Broccoli Soup with Garlic Croûtons.

2 medium onions.
2 oz (55 grams)/4 tblspns butter.
2 lbs (900 grams) broccoli.
2 pints (1.14 ltrs)/5 cups chicken stock.
Salt, pepper.
2 slices stale, white bread.
Clove garlic, crushed.
1 oz (30 grams)/2 tblspns butter.

Peel and chop onions. Soften in butter over a gentle heat. Add broccoli, turn over in the butter and onion. Add stock and seasoning. Cook gently for about 15 minutes. Put through sieve or purée in food processor. Thin if necessary with a little milk, check seasoning. Fry bread cubes in garlic and butter until golden brown. Serve soup very hot with the fried croûtons.

Hot Smoked Trout with Yoghurt and Herb Sauce.

1 trout per person, cleaned and filleted.
4 oz (110 grams)/½ cup natural yoghurt.
Fresh herbs.
Lemon juice.
Salt and pepper.
Cornflour, 1 tspn.

Use sea trout preferably. Rainbow trout will be quite successful also. If you have a home smoker use warm from smoker. If not, wrap trout in foil, with butter and seasoning and cook in a hot oven for 10 minutes.

Sauce: Put yoghurt into a heavy saucepan. Stablize by adding a tspn of cornflour. Bring slowly to boil, stirring in one direction only. Take off heat at once, add generous amount of chopped herbs (parsley, lemon balm, fennel), lemon juice, salt and pepper.

Cinnamon Apple Flan.

8 oz (225 grams)/1 2/3 cups plain flour.
Pinch salt.
6 oz (170 grams)/¾ cup butter.
2 egg yolks.
2 oz (55 grams)/¼ cup castor sugar.
2 tspns cinnamon.
3-4 firm eating apples.
Bailey's cream liqueur.
Brown sugar.

To make the sugar crust pastry sift in the cinnamon with the flour and castor sugar. Rub in the butter till it resembles fine breadcrumbs combine with the egg yolks. Mix to a dough. Leave to rest. Peel and slice apples neatly. Put in heavy saucepan with 2-3 tblspns liqueur. Cook very gently for 5 minutes. Roll out pastry, line an 8 inch (20 cm) flan tin with removable bottom. Place apples and liqueur in pastry case, add a little more liqueur if too dry. Sprinkle generously with brown sugar. Cook in a hot oven until pastry case is done and the sugar is caramelised. Serve with whipped cream.

The castle is a grey stone, turreted mansion built in 1876 by architect John Franklin Fuller. The drawings, without the baronial tower (an effective afterthought) are still in the house. Inside, all rooms open off a double height Gothic hall. It was bought by the late Major Robert Aldridge and his wife in 1932. Now run by Mrs. Aldridge.

Mount Falcon Castle

Mt. Falcon is above all a hotel with personality– that of the owner, Constance Aldridge who has managed it for over 50 years. Most of the guests are fisherfolk and shooters who return year after year. They fish all day and exchange fishy tales in the evening in the convivial atmosphere of the bar or library. If you are not a dedicated golfer or fisherperson you can sit in the beautiful garden, go sightseeing in Co. Mayo, or explore the pubs and shops in Ballina. The evening meal, served on the long mahogany table under the chandeliers is a truly baronial affair. Fish and game rank high on the menu and the milk, eggs and vegetables come from the castle farm. The bar is well stocked and run on a 'help yourself and sign the book' arrangement.

Mt Falcon Castle,
Ballina,
Co. Mayo.

Gravad Lax.

Clean and fillet about an 8 lb (3.6 kilo) salmon, if possible do not wash it.

6 level tblspns sugar.
6 level tblspns salt.
3 tblspns white pepper.
Plenty of dill.

Sprinkle the salt mixture on a sheet of greaseproof paper. Add a layer of dill stalks. Press more salt mixture onto the cut sides of both fillets, place one fillet on the greaseproof paper skin side down. Cover this with plenty of dill. Place the next fillet, cut side down, on top, sprinkle on the rest of the salt. Cover with dill and wrap the fish up in the greaseproof paper. Then wrap it all in a parcel of tin foil with a light weight on top. Put in a very cool place but not the fridge. Turn the fish once and leave for 48 hours.

It is now ready to eat. Carefully scrape off all the salt mixture and dill. Wipe it but do not wash it. Cut in thin slices like smoked salmon. Serve with dill sauce.

Jugged Hare.

As we have a constant supply of French shooters who give me hares to cook, this is their favourite dish. I make hare soup with the same flavourings which is also very popular.

1 hare cut off the bone (but left in large pieces). Keep the blood and liver.
2 oz (55 grams)/2 rashers streaky bacon.
Butter for frying.
Thyme, bay-leaf, parsley, cloves, peppercorns.
Marmalade.
Red wine.
Lemon juice if needed.
Onions

Boil up the bones for stock. Roll the meat in seasoned flour and brown in a little butter along with the onions and bacon. Take out the meat, add enough flour to soak up the fat. Add the stock and all the herbs, bring to the boil and stir for a few minutes. Pour this and the meat into a heavy casserole and boil for 2 hours on a slow heat until very tender. Add blood, mashed liver, red wine, marmalade and lemon juice if needed. I prefer wine and marmalade to port and redcurrant jelly. Keep tasting for the right flavour adding what ever is needed until it is just right.

Treacle Tart.

Bake blind a pastry case, preferably on a tin plate. In a small saucepan melt slightly- enough golden syrup to cover the pastry case, add a few drops of almond essence and a dash of lemon juice. Pour this into the case which has been filled with fine white bread crumbs. Make sure there are enough crumbs to exactly soak up the syrup so you can cut it without it being runny. Before eating sprinkle on a little ground almonds and a thin layer of crumbled cornflakes slightly crisp before serving.

Palladian House design by Francis Bindon built 1755-1774. It is Co. Sligo's most spectacular, surviving 18th century private house. Original four poster beds in all the bedrooms except one. Chests full of muslin dresses and brocades, all undisturbed through centuries of unbroken family ownership, still survive.

Coopershill House

Coopershill House has all the elegance of the Georgian era with the amenities of today. In the cooler evenings blazing fires and sparkling candelabra give a cheerful air and ponderous family portraits look down on the guests enjoying their nightcaps before retiring to their regal bedrooms. The extensive park, garden and working-farm make the perfect setting. Winner of the 1987 Good Hotel Guide Cesar Award for "Outstanding Irish Hospitality".

Coopershill House,
Coopershill,
Riverstown,
Co. Sligo.

Carrot & Orange Soup.

1 lb (450 grams)/3 cups carrots, chopped.
1 onion, chopped.
1½ pints (900 ml)/3¾ cups chicken stock.
1 tspn salt.
1 tspn sugar.
4 oranges, (juice only).
¼ pint (150 mls)/⅝ cup cream.
Chives.

Melt a little butter in a saucepan. Add carrots and onions and sauté till slightly soft. Pour in stock, add salt and sugar and simmer for about 1 hour. Liquidise and add strained orange juice. Decorate with whipped cream and chopped chives.

Chicken en Danse.

3¼-4 lb (1.6-1.8 kilos) roasting chicken.
Approx 3 tblspns flour.
8 oz (225 grams) green bacon, in one piece.
3 large Spanish onions.
1-2 cloves garlic.
1½ oz (45 grams)/3 tblspns butter.
3 tblspns of olive oil.
1 strip of dried orange peel.
2 cloves.
Fresh bouquet garni.
Coarse salt & freshly ground pepper.
5 fl. oz (150 ml)/⅝ cup of red wine.

Heat oven to 325°F/170°C/Regulo 3-4. Cut the chicken into 8 pieces. Dust with flour. Cut bacon into slices, ½ inch (15 mm) thick. Chop onions coarsely, flatten garlic with side of a knife. In a large casserole, sauté the bacon in the butter and olive oil until crisp and golden. Remove with a slotted spoon and reserve. Add chopped onions and sauté over low heat until soft and transparent. Remove with a slotted spoon and reserve. Add the chicken pieces to the casserole and sauté in two batches over a medium heat until golden. Return bacon pieces and onions to casserole. Add garlic, cloves, orange peel, bouquet garni and season to taste.

Cook in oven for 35-40 minutes or until chicken is tender. To finish pour the wine into a small saucepan and cook over a high heat until the wine is reduced to 4 tblspns (approx). Stir into casserole and serve immediately.

Fruit Crumble.

1½ lbs (675 grams) of blackberries & apples.
(gooseberries, rhubarb or plums may be used either).
4 oz (110 grams)/½ cup sugar.

Mix the prepared fruit and sugar. Turn into a 2-3 pint (1½-2 litre) greased dish.

Topping.

4 oz (110 grams)/1 scant cup flour.
2 oz (55 grams)/¼ cup butter.
4 oz (110 grams)/½ cup brown sugar.

Topping: Sift flour into a bowl and rub in the butter. Add the sugar. Continue to rub in until mixture resembles breadcrumbs. Sprinkle evenly over the fruit and press down slightly. Place in the centre of a moderate oven. Bake for 1 hour until golden brown. Dust with icing sugar. Serve with cream and/or icecream.

79

Drumlease Glebe House was built in 1834 for the cost of £900.00. It shares the more curious traits of many Irish Rectories. The formal front is sited to the garden. There is a Famine Wall enclosing a large garden. The entrance is a somewhat eccentric off centre porch, and an additional wing has been added to house the ever-increasing family of a mid-Victorian Rector.

Drumlease Glebe House

The drive from Sligo to Drumlease Glebe House is unforgettable. The green mountains and woods are reflected in the dark, mysterious water in the unspoilt countryside. This part of Ireland is a place of magnificent, untouched beauty. Round a few winding roads from all this I found Drumlease Glebe House tucked away in the middle of a forest with a river flowing past. Two donkeys gazed into space under a distant tree, a picture of serenity and peace.

Barbara and Andrew Greenstein, came here from America in 1986 with their dog "Poteen", when they bought this gentle and mellow mansion. The high-ceilinged bedrooms are comfortably furnished, prettily wallpapered and the beds covered with Laura Ashley quilts. The dining-room is open to residents only as is the swimming pool in the garden.

Drumlease Glebe House,
Dromahair,
Co. Leitrim.

Tomato Ice-Cream with Prawns.

An unusual starter. It can be served on its own with brown bread and orange butter but we embellish it with prawns. No mayonnaise is required. If the tomatoes are not quite the best, use a pinch of sugar to help the flavour.

2 huge, or 3 large tomatoes,
Juice of ½ lemon,
Tomato ketchup to taste or tomato concentrate,
4 fl.oz. (125ml cream)/½ cup whipped double cream,
Salt and pepper,
Curry powder to taste if desired,
10-12 prawns,
1 thinly sliced lemon for garnish.

Put the tomatoes through a mouli or blender, then sieve to eliminate any last trace of skin. Add the remaining ingredients in the given order. Freeze at the lowest possible temperature until firm.

To serve: use a small cold ice cream scoop. Place two small or one large scoop of the tomato ice cream on a large lettuce leaf. Garnish with prawns and a twisted lemon slice.

Orange Butter

1lb (450 grams)/2 cups butter at room temperature,
1 orange, grated for zest and squeezed for juice.

Blend butter and orange zest in a food processor until soft. Add orange juice gradually and blend.

This keeps very well, any quantity desired may be made.

Pack in a small crockery bowl. Make a circular design on top using the prongs of a fork. Serve chilled with a bright flower blossom for garnish.

Fillet of Beef Drumlease

Since we are Americans, it seemed appropriate to use this rich but wonderful recipe for beef fillet.

René Verdon was the White House chef during the Kennedy administration. It is his recipe for echalotte butter that is used between thin slices of fillet steak (U.S. Fillet mignon). The butter melts as the steak is cooked, flavouring the meat and giving it a wonderful moistness.

2½-3lb (1.25kg) fillet of beef, trimmed.
1 tblspn sunflower oil.

Meat Preparation

Trim the fillet. Heat oil in a well seasoned frying pan and when very hot, add beef. Turn on all sides until sealed and brown. Remove and cool. Cut into thin ½ inch (1cm) vertical slices leaving it attached at the base of the fillet. (Allow 4-5 slices person).

Echalotte Butter.

1 tblspn shallots, chopped.
2 tblspns dry white wine.

Place the above ingredients in a small saucepan and cook over a moderate heat until white wine has almost evaporated and shallots are soft.

4oz (110 grams)/½ cup butter.
1 tblspn fresh parsley, chopped.
2 cloves garlic, crushed.
Salt and pepper, to taste.
3 tblspns breadcrumbs.
1oz (30 grams)/¼ cup gruyere cheese, grated.
Pinch of nutmeg.

Blend all ingredients in a food processor until thoroughly combined. Spread some of the echalotte butter between each slice and on top. Tie cotton string around the beef to secure it. Place beef on an ungreased tray with edges or in a dish. Bake in a moderate oven, (not hot, or the butter will brown). Cook according to thickness of beef. (A smaller joint of 1½-2lb/675-900 grams will take 40 minutes in a 400°F/200°C/Regulo 6 oven allowing 20 minutes per pound/450 grams). Remove, let stand for 5-10 minutes covered by foil. Remove string, cut slices through and fan down vertically on a heated plate with a large piece of lettuce and carved tomato rose at the top. Spoon excess butter (reheated) over the meat, as much of the melts out. (Any left-over butter can be refrigerated to firm and spread over vegetables at another meal). Do not "cremate" the beef while cooking – the centre should be rare to medium-rare for best flavour and effect. Check between slices during cooking.

Colcannon.

We like to serve some traditional old Irish recipes. This is one of the oldest and gets its name from "cal (kale or cabbage)" and "ceann thionn (white headed)" in Irish.

6 large potatoes, peeled and boiled.
6 shallots/spring onions.
5 fl.oz (150ml)/⅝ cup sour cream.
8 oz (225 grams) curly kale or leaf cabbage, (cooked).
2 oz (55 grams)/¼ cup butter.
1 tblspn chopped parsley.
Salt and pepper.

Mash potatoes finely, add chopped onions to the milk with salt and pepper. Infuse the milk by boiling. Chop cabbage finely and add half the butter. Fold all together and beat hard. Serve with a well of butter in the centre.

Pears Eileen Joyce

6 firm pears with stems, nicely shaped.
8oz (225 grams)/1 cup sugar.
12 fl. oz (370 ml)/1½ cups water.
4 fl. oz (120 ml)/½ cup Crème de Menthe.
2 cinnamon sticks.
6 cloves.
Juice of 1 lemon.
4oz (110 grams) good dark chocolate.
2oz (55 grams)/4 tblspns unsalted butter.
1 tblspn rum.
Garnish: double cream, whipped to piping consistency; candied violets.

Boil sugar and water together for 2 minutes. Add Crème de Menthe, cinnamon, cloves and lemon. Leave to keep hot on top of cooker while you are preparing the pears.

Peel pears, keeping stems intact. Cut a small slice off bottom of each pear so it remains upright. Place immediately into the hot prepared syrup. Poach until soft but firm enough to retain shape well. Cool and soak overnight if possible. Prepare chocolate coating by melting chocolate and butter over simmering water in a double boiler. Add rum. Wipe cold pears dry (important!), dip into warm chocolate mixture or spoon mixture over pears. It must be of a pourable consistency–not too thick and not too thin for best adherence.

After pear is completely covered (except stem), drain off excess chocolate and place in centre of dessert plate and allow to cool. Just before serving, using star shaped nozzle, pipe stiffly whipped cream along base of pear creating a "nest effect". Place 3 crystallised violets on the cream to decorate.

Note: Pear poaching liquid may be strained and stored in a closed container for several weeks in the fridge for re-use.

Knockmuldowney

T his old house, not very big, sandwiched between Ballisodare Bay and Knocknarea Mountain, is in an attractive garden setting. It was restored in 1982 by Charles and Mary Cooper and run as a restaurant. It has an impressive wine list (The house has a rather alcoholic history!–see footnote) and has quickly gained a very good local reputation. It was expanded into a small hotel in 1985. The colours in the bedrooms are fresh and bright. The rooms are large, very comfortable and would be hard to fault. I woke up to the spectacular view of the Ox Mountains, the bay and the little stone boat-house which doesn't ever quite reach the water.

Knockmuldowney,
Culleenamore,
Nr Strandhill,
Co. Sligo.

Built in 1820 as the seaside retreat of the Cockburns– Sligo Wine Merchants. Later acquired by the Jameson's of Irish whiskey fame who laid out much of the garden. On the lawn is a little cat cemetry, last resting place of "Coco" and "Judy" erected by Major General McCalmont in 1950 and 1953.

Melon in Elderflower Wine.

1 good ripe melon.
½ pint (300 ml)/1¼ cups elderflower wine.
6 borage flowers, (if available).

Peel and seed the melon, slice thinly and put it in a flat dish. Cover with the elderflower wine and refrigerate for at least four hours. Before serving arrange the melon in individual plates and pour over some of the juice. Garnish with borage flowers.

Elderflower Wine.

Most home wine-making books include a recipe for this– make sure not to use elderberry wine. Any sauternes type wines may be substituted.

Marinated Lamb Kebab & Mint Hollandaise.

3 lb (1.35 kilos) leg of lamb cut into 1" (2½ cm) cubes.
1 green pepper, cut into 1" (2½ cm) squares.
1 red pepper, cut into 1" (2½ cm) squares.
6 tomatoes, halved.
12 mushroom caps.

Marinade.

1 bay leaf.
1 onion diced.
1 clove garlic, finely chopped.
Pinch cumin seed.
½ pint (300 ml)/10 fl. oz olive oil.
Salt and black pepper.

Put the lamb cubes with all the marinade ingredients in a bowl for at least 8 hours. When ready to cook, arrange the lamb cubes on skewers alternately with the peppers, mushrooms and tomatoes. Cook over charcoal or under a grill turning frequently until cooked. Serve with mint hollandaise and rice.

Mint Hollandaise.

4 large egg yolks.
8 oz (225 grams)/1 cup unsalted butter.
4 tblspns white vinegar.
1 tblspn fresh mint, (chopped).
Small pinch salt.

Boil vinegar and reduce by half. Melt butter over a moderate heat. Whisk the egg yolks in a bowl over hot water with vinegar and salt. Slowly add the butter, whisk until of a thick, creamy sauce-like texture. If it's too thick add a little warm water.
(*Note:* Food processors make a good hollandaise). Finally add mint, stir and serve with kebabs.

Bailey's Blackberry Mist.

8 oz (225 grams)/2 cups blackberries.
¼ oz (7.5 grams)/1 tblspn gelatine.
2 tblspns water.
½ pint (300 ml)/1¼ cups cream.
2 tblspns Bailey's Cream liqueur.
2 egg whites.
4 tblspns castor sugar.

Liquidize the blackberries. Put through a sieve to remove all the pips. Dissolve gelatine in water. To the purée add Bailey's Irish Cream and sugar. Whip the cream and fold into the purée. Add more sugar if required as blackberries can vary a lot in sweetness. Whip egg-whites and fold into mixture with the gelatine. Cool before serving.

Rathmullan House was the seaside residence of the Batt family. A regency villa of 1837 vintage, doubled in size in 1880 so that there are two front doors. An equally amiable excentric interior culminates in a Hindu Gothic dining-room recalling the family sojourn in India. The spacious gardens slope down through rare trees to a sandy beach with a view of the mountains across the lough. Interior decoration of the house is by the present owners, Robin and Bob Wheeler.

Rathmullan House

The most northerly of the Country Houses–(you can't get much further north than Lough Swilly). County Donegal is one of Ireland's most beautiful counties. The garden at Rathmullan is a joy, lovingly cared for by generations of Irish men and women. With the view from the dining room it is hard to concentrate on your plate. The food is traditional and super-abundant, with salmon, trout, Donegal lamb and beef much in evidence. Beautiful food eaten in beautiful surroundings. The hotel is one of the largest of the Country House Hotels and is a relaxed and comfortable place for a long or short stay.

Rathmullan House,
Rathmullan,
Co. Donegal.

Mushroom Croustades.

For 24 croustades

These are small breadcases with a delicious filling of mushrooms. They need to be prepared in advance and made ready to put in the oven ten minutes before being served. I use a food processor to chop the shallots/onions and mushrooms. They will keep quite happily in a warm oven for 20-30 minutes.

Breadcases.

For 24 bun tins

12 slices white bread.
1 oz (30 grams)/2 tblspns soft butter.

Coat the inside of a bun sheet with butter. Using a 2½ inch (6.5 cm) cutter make two rounds from each slice of bread. Press firmly and neatly into each bun tin. Bake in a preheated oven, 400°F/200°C/Reg 6 for 10 minutes. Cool on a wire rack. Any not used will keep in an air tight tin.

The Filling.

2 oz (55 grams)/¼ cup butter.
3 tblspns shallots/spring onions, finely chopped.
½ lb (225 grams)/2½ cups mushrooms, finely chopped.
2 level tblspns flour.
½ pint (300 ml)/1¼ cups cream.
½ tspn salt.
Pinch cayenne.
1 tblspn chopped parsley.
1½ tblspns chopped chives.
½ tspn lemon juice.
Little grated parmesan cheese.
Butter.

Melt butter in frying pan, cook shallots/spring onions for about 5 minutes without browning. Add mushrooms and stir well. Allow to cook until all the moisture has evaporated. Remove pan from heat. Mix the flour in well and add the cream. Stir continuously and bring to the boil for a minute or two. Off the heat, add the seasonings, herbs and lemon juice. Turn into a bowl and refrigerate for at least 4 hours.

To serve: Fill each case. Sprinkle with a little parmesan cheese. Dot with the extra butter. Place on baking sheet and heat in preset oven 350°F/180°C/Reg 4 for 10 minutes.

The filling will keep for 2-3 days well-covered in the fridge.

Gooseberry Sorbet.

I keep a jar of Baumé (stock syrup) made up in the fridge. I also freeze gooseberries in 1 lb 2 oz (500 grams) lots for using later in the year.

17½ fl. oz (545 mls) 2 cups water.
1 lb 2 oz (500 grams)/2¼ cups sugar.
1 lb 2 oz (500 grams) gooseberries.
1 egg white.

Bring the sugar and water to the boil gently making sure the sugar is dissolved. Boil for 1 minute. Stew gooseberries in a little water until soft. Liquidize and rub through a fine sieve. Mix with syrup. Add white of egg and churn in an ice cream maker. Alternatively place mixture without white of egg in deep freeze and leave until slushy. Add stiffly beaten white of egg and return to freezer.

Poached Salmon.

Nowadays salmon is available all year round with the marketing of farm-bred fish. Spring salmon is still the finest for flavour. We like to serve it just warm or to make sure it has had time to soften after refrigeration.

To cook we make up a salmon bath of water with salt, peppercorns, parsley stalks, thinly sliced onion and lemon, sliced carrot and celery, bay leaves, thyme and fennel, simmer for 5 minutes. The fish is placed in the bath and poached with hardly any movement of the liquid. A 10 lb (4.5 kilo) fish takes approx 1¼ hours.

Later in the season we add olive oil to the water when the salmon tends to get drier. The salmon can be served with a herb hollandaise, mayonnaise, or brown butter. Excellent served with new potatoes and a salad.

Little Chocolate Pots.

We use the small "pot au chocolat" for this pudding, but any small dishes will do. They do need to be small, as this is a very rich mousse.

12 oz (340 grams) dark chocolate.
6 tblspns water.
1 oz (30 grams)/2 tblspns butter.
2 dessrtspns rum.
6 eggs (separated).

Melt the chocolate and water over low heat. Add butter and rum off the heat. Separate 6 eggs and add each yolk separately, stirring in well. Whisk the egg whites to firm snow and stir in briskly. Fill containers, we use a jug for this. Keep for a day before using. They will keep for at least a week in the fridge. The chocolate needs to be the best dark chocolate you can get.

Blackheath House was built as the Glebe House of the parish of St. Guaire in 1795 by the Earl Bishop of Bristol, for one of his nephews. It is attributed to Cork architect Michael Shanahan. The facade of two stories conceals a structure of four floors– a compact and commodious plan characteristic of Irish rectories. Acquired by Joseph and Margaret Erwin and restored by them in 1978 first as a private house and later converted into a country house hotel and restaurant.

Blackheath House

Blackheath House remained in church hands for 100 years before being bought as a private estate by the Rothwell family. Its heyday appears to have been during the long encumbancies of the Rev. Alexander followed by his son-in-law Dean Andrew Smyly covering the years 1832-1880. Rev Alexander became Primate of All Ireland and his wife Cecil (1818-1895) a noted poet, wrote many famous hymns including–"There is a Green Hill Far Away", "All Things Bright and Beautiful", and "Once in Royal David's City".

The hotel-restaurant (MacDuffs) is situated within the six counties of Northern Ireland adjacent to the scenic coastline of Londonderry and the Giant's Causeway. The bedrooms are stylish and endowed with colour television and ensuite bathrooms–(amenities I am sure the 18th century rectors would have frowned upon). The food and service however reflect the standards of past centuries with local game, seafood and fresh garden and farm produce cooked with great care something which is rare in these hurried times.

Blackheath House,
112 Killeague Road,
Blackhill,
Coleraine,
Co. Londonderry.

Prawn Puffs.

1 lb (450 grams) cooked prawns.
¾ lb (340 grams) puff pastry.
Seasoning.

Roll out the pastry finely. Using a tea plate cut six round shapes. Cover half the pastry with prawns and seasoning, fold over top to make a semi-circle and press edges together with a little water. Turn until the fluted edge is on top like a pasty, coat with beaten egg. Cook in a hot oven for ten minutes or until pastry is cooked. Serve at once with a side salad garnish and cold savoury sauces. For example, tartare sauce, Marie Rose, or Ohio Sauce (as below).

Ohio Sauce.

1 large onion.
1 lb (450 grams) jar preserved beetroot.
2 tblspns mayonnaise.
2 oz (55 grams)/¼ cup Philadelphia cheese.
Cream.

Cut and boil onion in the vinegar from beetroot jar, then add the beetroot, purée in a food processor with the Philadelphia. Then add the mayonnaise and a little cream to taste. Will keep well in a covered container if refrigerated.

Rack of Lamb with Mulled Wine Sauce.

2 racks of lamb, enough to give three cutlets per person.

Have the butcher cut through the bone. Cut six joints of three cutlets each. Remove fat from bone end of joint and score the remainder in a criss-cross pattern. Cook on a tray in a hot oven for 10 minutes to crisp the fat and then in a moderate oven until the meat is cooked to your preference. Carve each joint and serve on individual plates decorated with fresh herbs, mulled wine sauce and seasonal fruits. e.g. redcurrants, plums, or blackberries.

Mulled Wine Sauce.

4 tblspns redcurrant jelly.
2 tblspns port.
2 glasses red wine.
½ tspn cinnamon.
½ tspn ginger.
½ tspn nutmeg.
Juice of 1 lemon.
Juice of 1 orange.

Combine all ingredients together in a saucepan and let simmer until the jelly has melted. Continue to cook until the mixture is reduced by half and has a good flavour. If further thickening is required use a little arrowroot and water.

Athol Brose.

A Scottish dessert of which there are many variations.

1 pint (600 ml)/2 ½ cups stiffly whipped cream.
3 tblspns soft runny honey.
2 tblspns muesli.
4 tblspns whisky–or to taste.

Gently fold in muesli with the cream, add the honey and lastly the whisky. Stir carefully. Transfer to individual glasses. Decorate with toasted oatmeal. Chill and serve with flakemeal biscuits.

Flakemeal Biscuits.

4 oz (110 grams)/ ½ cup margarine.
2 oz (55 grams)/ ¼ cup sugar.
2 oz (55 grams)/ ½ cup flour.
½ teaspoon salt.
5 oz (140 grams)/ 1 1/3 cups flakemeal, (porridge oats).
Pinch of bicarbonate soda.

Mix all ingredients in a food processor. Roll out and cut biscuits into required shapes. Bake at 350-375°F/180-190°C/Regulo 4-5 for approximately 20 minutes. Sprinkle with sugar.

The origin of the building is uncertain but the house which Samuel bought was burnt down in 1800 and rebuilt over the next 15 years. John Madden, great grandfather of the present John Madden, was responsible for digging out the basement, facing the exterior with Dungannon stone and for the sinking of the 132 foot well. An extensive traveller, he added fir and sequoia trees to the park which he brought as seed from North America. These can still be seen today.

Hilton Park
"Mighty oaks from little acorns grow"

H ilton Park was bought by Rev. Samuel Madden in 1732 for his son, whose bride brought a bag of acorns from her old home to her new one. From these acorns grew the oak wood which you can see at Hilton today. Samuel Madden, a distinguished man of letters and friend of Dr. Johnson, was variously a founder member of the Royal Dublin Society, Rector of Newtownbutler, tutor to Frederick, Prince of Wales and benefactor of Trinity College where he endowed Premiums for the advancement of learning from which he earned the sobriquet 'Premium'. Madden was an expert on apple and pear trees. His best known books are 'Reflections and Resolutions proper for the Gentlemen of Ireland' and 'A Memoir of the 20th Century' written well over 150 years before its commencement.

When you arrive at Hilton Park you immediately feel how fortunate you are to have found it. It is quite delightful, a very large and handsome country house with a garden, park, farm and splendid countryside all around. The bedrooms are all individual in style and the reception rooms splendidly furnished. The food is fresh local produce and mostly from the farm including the cream cheeses. There was a full Irish breakfast, but I had just the porridge with fresh cream and honey which was a feast to start the day.

Hilton Park,
Scotshouse,
Clones,
Co. Monaghan.

Pike Quenelles.

8 oz (225 grams) pike (free of all bones and skin).
1 large egg white.
8 fl. oz (250 ml)/1 cup cream.
Salt & pepper.
Fish stock or lightly salted water for poaching.
¾ pint (450 ml)/2 scant cups fish stock.
1 tblspn white wine.
3 tblspns double cream.
Grated cheese.

Put the pike into a food processer and purée. Season with the pepper, add the egg white, purée again. Put this mixture into a glass or metal bowl, press down over the surface with cling film and place in a larger bowl containing crushed ice. Leave in the refrigerator for 1 hour. Remove, beat in a little more cream and return to the refrigerator for 15 minutes, repeating the process until half the cream is left. Whip the remaining cream, season with salt and beat into the fish purée. Gently poach dessertspoonfuls of the mixture in simmering fish stock or water for about 5 minutes.

To prepare the sauce. Boil and reduce the fish stock until thick. Add wine and cream to taste, then season. Pour over the quenelles, sprinkle with a little grated cheese and glaze under a grill.

Fillet of Lamb en croûte with Francatelli Sauce.

3 fillets of lamb, cut from 3 best ends and trimmed of all fat.
2 oz (55 grams)/¼ cup butter.
A few spinach leaves,
Black pepper.
1 lb (450 grams) puff pastry.

Francatelli Sauce.

½ lb (225 grams)/¾ cup redcurrant jelly.
3 tblspns port.
Small stick cinnamon, bruised.
Thinly pared zest of lemon.

Melt the butter in a saucepan and quickly seal the lamb fillets. Remove and cool. Season and wrap the spinach leaves around the fillets. Roll out the pastry as thinly as will hold and wrap around the spinach covered fillets. Brush with beaten egg and cook in a hot oven. 425°F/220°C/Regulo 7 for 15-20 minutes. Allow the meat to stand for 5 minutes before slicing into six pieces. Just before you take the meat out of the oven, put all the ingredients for the sauce in a pan and heat gently. Allow to simmer for 5 minutes while the meat is standing. Serve with green vegetables in season.

Steamed Chocolate Pudding.

4 oz (110 grams)/½ cup butter or margarine.
4 oz (110 grams)/½ cup castor sugar.
Extra 4 oz (110 grams)/½ cup castor sugar. (for meringue)
1 oz (30 grams)/4 level tblspns cocoa powder.
Scant ¼ pint/(140 mls)/½ cup milk.
2 eggs.

Cream the fat and sugar. Separate the eggs, beat the yolks with the milk. Add to the creamed mixture with the flour and the cocoa powder. Butter a bowl, put in the pudding mixture, secure well with greaseproof paper and steam for about 1½ hours. When the pudding is cooked, remove from the bowl and cover with a meringue made from the egg whites and extra castor sugar. Brown gently in a hot oven.

Moyglare Manor.

This elegant Georgian House has been handsomely furnished with a profusion of antiques, paintings and oriental rugs by owner Norah Devlin. The main drawing room, with plaster work ceiling (attributed to Michael Stapleton) and rich burgundy red walls, is a particularly lovely room. Each bedroom is immaculately kept, comfortably furnished with antiques and carefully chosen fabrics. Here I saw a lady on her hands and knees combing rug frills to make sure they were straight! There is a club-like bar with a blazing fire which is a focal point for guests but there are many other small public rooms for those who prefer solitude. The restaurant is fully licenced and the food highly recommended. Maynooth is an historic university and market town in Co. Kildare, Ireland's world famous horse breeding and training county. The rural bliss of Moyglare is only 18 miles from Dublin.

Moyglare Manor,
Maynooth,
Co. Kildare.

Moyglare Manor, built in 1775 is supposedly the Dower House to the nearby Carton Estate. It was bought as a family home and refurbished as an hotel in the last five years by owner Norah Devlin.

Carrot and Onion Soup.

3 lb (1.4 kilos) carrots.
2 lb (900 grams) potatoes.
1 onion.
8 fl. oz (250 ml)/1 cup fresh orange juice.
4 pints (2.4 litres)/10 cups chicken stock.
1 pint (600 ml)/2½ cups milk or milk and cream.
2 ozs (55 grams)/¼ cup butter.
Salt and pepper.

Roughly chop all vegetables. Sweat in melted butter for 10 minutes. Add chicken stock and seasoning. Cook until vegetables are soft. Liquidise, add orange juice and return to heat. Blend in milk and cream.

Pigeon Pie.

Puff pastry.
6 pigeon breasts.
10 oz (300 grams) of beef.
6 oz (170 grams) of streaky bacon.
¼ pint (150 ml)/⅝ cup of red wine.
½ pint (300 ml)/1¼ cups of chicken stock.
Sprig of thyme & parsley.
2 cloves garlic.
1 large onion, chopped.
¼ pint (150 grams) tomato purée.
3 tblspns, vegetable oil.

Slice beef and pigeon breasts into ½ inch (1¼ cm) strips. Slice the bacon, onion and crush the garlic. Toss all in a heavy casserole with oil for about five minutes. Remove from pan and add wine, stock and tomato purée. Reduce for about 2 minutes. Add all ingredients and season. Cover and place in a moderate oven for one hour. Remove from oven, thicken with an ounce of roux, place in oven dish, cover with puff pastry and return to oven for 15 minutes.

Chocolate Profiteroles with Banana Cream.
Choux Pastry

3-4 eggs.
2 oz (55 grams)/¼ cup butter.
8 fl. oz (250 ml)/1 cup water.
5 oz (140 grams)/1 cup flour.

Filling.

5 fl. oz (150 ml) 2/3 cup whipped cream.
1 banana liquidised.
Juice of ½ lemon.
Brandy to taste.

Icing.

4 oz (110 grams) chocolate.
Stock Syrup
Brandy to taste.

For pastry. Bring butter and water almost to boil, add the flour and cook for 1½ minutes stirring all the time, gradually beat in eggs until consistency is thick and shiny. Using a ⅜ nozzle, put mixture in piping bag and pipe into small profiterole shapes on a lightly greased baking tray. Cook at 350°F/180°C/Reg 4 for 20 minutes, prick pastry and return to oven for a further 5-10 minutes until dried out. Remove and allow to cool.

Filling: Blend all ingredients and pipe into profiteroles. Stack on a plate.

Icing: Melt chocolate, add enough syrup to make a creamy consistency and add brandy to taste. Pour over profiteroles.

Restaurants

The Step House Restaurant

The Step House is sited opposite, and was formerly part of, the estate of the MacMurragh Kavanaghs—once Kings of Leinster. It was possibly by the architect William Morrison c. 1820. A gothic front door gives access to Greek Revival Interior and the windows overlook the imposing entrance gates of the estate.

The descendants of the MacMurragh Kavanaghs still live in Borris. One of the more famous members of the family in the last century was Arthur who, though born limbless, learned to ride, fish, shoot and sail. He travelled alone to Egypt, Scandinavia, Russia and India. He had a sojourn to the Palace of Westminster as M.P. for Carlow for 12 years. He also married and had children. He was ill in Persia and nursed back to health in the harem of a Persian Prince. Arthur's daughter Agnes died at the Step-House in the Autumn of 1930. The Coady family purchased the house after Agnes's death and turned it into a restaurant. With such a history I expected a warm and interesting place with charm and personality and it certainly lived up to my expectations. The food and wine were excellent.

Artichauts Farci.

4-6 artichokes.
4 oz (110 grams)/1 cup crab meat.
4 oz (110 grams)/1 cup prawns.

Dressing.

½ or 1 small green pepper, chopped.
10 fl. oz (300 ml)/½ pint mayonnaise flavoured with grated lemon rind.
2 tblspns snipped chives & parsley or spring onion.
Salt.
Ground, black pepper.

Trim off the points of the leaves of the artichokes with scissors and trim the stalk from the bottom. Cook the artichokes in boiling salted water until a leaf can be pulled out, about 35-40 minutes. Drain, refresh and leave until cold. Meanwhile, prepare the dressing. Drop the green pepper into boiling water, cook for 1 minute, then drain and dry. Mix the mayonnaise with lemon juice and sugar. Add the green pepper and herbs or spring onion to the dressing. Pull out the centre leaves from each artichoke and scrape away the 'choke'. Mix the flaked crab meat with the prawns and moisten with the dressing. Put a spoonful of the crab mixture in the centre of each artichoke. Serve cold.

Chicken Valencia with Pine Nuts.

4 large chicken breasts, split lengthways and beaten flat.
2 tblspns oil.
1 tblspn butter.
4 fl. oz (125 ml)/½ cup Cointreau.
2 oranges.
4 tspns Dijon mustard.
3 tblspns cultured sour cream.
1 tspn fresh thyme.
2 fl. oz (60 ml)/¼ cup chicken stock.
Sea salt & freshly ground black pepper.
2 dessertspns pine nuts, lightly toasted.

Toss chicken in seasoned flour. Put oil in copper pan, when very hot add the chicken, reduce heat and lightly brown for 2-4 minutes each side (depending on the thickness). Discard the oil in the pan, remove the chicken and keep warm. Retain any sediment in pan and add the liquor, flame reduce to a syrup–don't allow the pan to overheat at this stage. Add mustard, sour cream, thyme, 2 tspns finely grated orange rind, salt and pepper. Return pan to low heat with the chicken and stock. Cook for 2-5 minutes. Arrange on plate with nuts tossed on top and garnish with the peeled orange slices. Serve with new potatoes.

Framboise.

6 oz (170 grams) rich shortcrust pastry.
1 lb (450 grams) fresh or frozen raspberries.
3 egg whites.
6 oz (170 grams)/¾ cup sugar.
3 oz (85 grams)/2/3 cup almonds, (freshly blanched and ground, but not oiled).
1 tblspn flaked almonds.

Line 10 inch (25 cm) flan ring with the pastry. Bake blind (if using fresh raspberries) for about 15 minutes, this is not necessary if using still frozen raspberries. Whisk the egg whites until stiff but not dry, then add 1 tblspn of measured sugar and whisk for one minute. Cut and fold in the remaining sugar and ground almonds. Fill the flan with the raspberries and top with the meringue mixture making sure to cover all the fruit. Toss the flaked almonds on top. Bake at 350°F (180°C)/Reg 4 for 30-40 minutes. If meringue starts to brown reduce heat, it shouldn't be any darker than a very light biscuit colour. Serve straight from oven with lightly whipped fresh cream.

Step House Restaurant,
Borris,
Co. Carlow.

Doyle's Schoolhouse Restaurant.

An interesting example of an Irish village school now remodelled principally as a restaurant but with four bedrooms with ensuite bathrooms upstairs. The village is of great historical interest with its round tower, Celtic Crosses, and Norman Arch. The remains of St. John's Friary, at one time a noted leper hospital, is across the road from the restaurant. The most recent historical treasure (unearthed in 1967) is a Viking stone known as a Hogback, the only known one in Ireland.

John Doyle, an enthusiastic cook, returned from "foreign parts" to his own village to start Doyle's Schoolhouse Restaurant in 1975. The sophisticated menu contains many Irish favourites. It has great local appeal but sadly it is often missed by tourists.

Lambs Brains Schoolhouse Style.

6 sets lambs brains.

Batter:
4 oz (110 grams)/1 cup flour.
1 oz (30 grams)/2 tblspn butter.
1 tblspn brandy.
2 egg whites.
Salt, pepper.
Warm water.

Sauce:
8 hard-boiled egg yolks.
13 fl. oz (400 ml)/1⅝ cup olive oil.
Juice of 1 lemon.
2 tspns capers, (chopped).
Salt, pepper.

Prepare the batter by melting the butter and adding it with enough warm water to the flour to make it the texture of heavy cream. Mix in the brandy. Season and fold in the egg whites. Rest for 1 hour. Slice the brains into medallions. Dip into the batter and deep fry until golden brown.

Sauce.

Blend the yolks, and lemon juice in a liquidizer, add a little oil and blend until emulsified. Incorporate all the oil. Stir in the capers.

Pigeon breast with Lime and Peppery Pineapple.

Ingredients per person:

4 pigeon breasts.
4 small tomatoes, (optional).
Watercress leaves, (optional).
Butter for cooking.

For the sauce:
34 fl. oz (1.060 litres) pigeon stock.
5½ oz (155 grams)/⅝ cup granulated sugar.
5 fl. oz (160 ml)/⅝ cup white vinegar.
Juice of 4 limes.
Salt and pepper.

For the pineapple.
2 pineapple slices.
6½ tblspns white wine vinegar.
3½ tblspns red wine vinegar.
6 tblspns granulated sugar.
2 tblspns whole peppercorns.

Candied zest.
Zest of 4 limes.
Zest of 4 lemons.
Equal amounts of sugar and water.

Sauce: place the vinegar and sugar in a small saucepan. Boil until the mixture begins to caramelise. Add the lime juice and cook 10 minutes, then add the pigeon stock and cook slowly, uncovered for at least one hour to reduce. Season with salt and pepper as needed. Reserve. Remove the pineapple rind and any hard spots in the pulp. Cut the pineapple in half lengthwise, then halve each piece lengthwise. Remove the central core. Save any juice that comes from the fruit. Cut into large chunks. Place both vinegars, peppercorns, and sugar in a saucepan and simmer for 30 minutes. Add the pineapple and continue cooking for 20 minutes. Remove from heat and set aside. Cut the lime and orange zest into julienne strips. Make a sugar syrup by bringing the sugar and water to the boil without stirring. Cook the strips in the syrup until softened and they have become candied. Set aside. Heat a little butter in a frying pan and cook the pigeon breasts over low heat for 12-15 minutes (they should only be rare).

To serve: Spoon some sauce onto each plate. Slice the pigeon breasts and place on top of the sauce. Spoon a little sauce over the meat, then sprinkle the candied zest over. Place some of the pineapple on each plate and decorate (if desired) with a tomato cut like a flower on some fresh watercress leaves, and serve.

Walnut and Almond Gâteaux.

12 oz (340 grams)/1½ cups sugar.
7 eggs.
4 oz (110 grams)/1 cup walnuts, chopped.
4 oz (110 grams)/½ cup almonds, ground.
1 tspn vanilla extract.
3 oz (85 grams)/¾ cup cornflour.
10 fl. oz (300 ml)/1¼ cups whipped cream, sweetened.
6½ oz (200 ml) coffee flavoured 'crème anglaise'.

Mix together the sugar, 1 whole egg and 6 egg yolks. Beat well so that a smooth paste is obtained. Add the walnuts, ground almonds, vanilla and cornflour. Gently incorporate the stiffly beaten egg-whites with the other ingredients. Pour into a buttered and floured cake tin. Bake in a moderate oven for 35 minutes. Let cool and cut into layers. Spread each layer with whipped cream. Place the layers on top of each other and coat the top with the coffee-flavoured crème anglaise.

Doyle's Schoolhouse Restaurant,
Castledermot,
Co. Kildare.

Galley

The "St. Ciaran" started life as the first non steam passenger boat on the Norfolk Broads. As the "Wroxham Belle" it did war service patrolling the Broads, when it looked as though invasion was imminent, during the second World War. After a few years in Sierra Leone, it was brought home to work on the Thames. In 1956 it was bought by the Irish Government to work on the Shannon. Dick Fletcher purchased the boat in 1964 and now operates it as a cruising restaurant on the rivers Nore and Barrow. The scenic valleys of these two rivers abound with Medieval Castles and Abbeys.

O nly in Ireland would you find a boat on a list of country houses! The "St. Ciaran" is a fully licensed cruising restaurant, seating 85 people, which operates out of New Ross. Peter Denny, the on board chef, trained at Ballymaloe and worked in Paris in "La Ferme Irlandaise" (the Irish restaurant).

Galley Tomato & Mint Soup.

1 1/3 pints (800 ml)/3 ½ cups tomatoe purée.
8 fl. oz (250 ml)/1 cup white sauce.
8 fl. oz (250 ml)/1 cup chicken stock.
1 tblspn chopped onions.
Butter.
Mint.
4 fl. oz (120 ml)/½ cup cream.
Salt & pepper.
1 or 2 tspns sugar.

To make tomato purée, put very ripe tomatoes to heat slowly without water until soft. Rub through a sieve. Add white sauce and stock to the hot purée. Season to taste adding a little sugar if the soup is bitter. Bring to the boil. Sweat the onions in the butter and add to soup stirring in the mint and some cream, chives or thyme if desired.

Chicken à l'Arlène.

1 medium sized chicken.
4 oz (110 grams) sausage meat.
4 oz (110 grams)/2 cups fresh breadcrumbs.
1 medium sized onion (diced).
2 oz (55 grams)/¼ cup butter, (melted).
1 tblspn mixed herbs including: thyme, parsley, marjarom and chives.

Bone the chicken completely keeping the meat intact in the skin. Make the stuffing by sweating the onion in the melted butter, add the sausage meat and the breadcrumbs, finally add the mixed herbs. Roll the stuffing into a cylinder and wrap the chicken around the stuffing, you may need to tie the roll. Cook at 400°F/200°C/Regulo 6 for about 1 hour.

Lemon and Honey Meringue Pie.

6 lemons.
6 oz (170 grams)/½ cup honey.
3¼ fl. oz (115 ml) water.
2¾ oz (85 grams)/½ cup plain flour.
6 eggs.
8 oz (225 grams)/1 cup sugar.
Sweet shortcrust pastry.

Separate the eggs. Peel the lemons, put peelings in boiling water and leave for 4 minutes off the heat. Strain the water and keep to one side. Squeeze the lemons mix the juice with the water and blend in the flour. Bring this to the boil. When it begins to thicken, add honey and then the egg yolks. Stir until everything is blended and leave to cool. Make a shortcrust sweet pastry and line a flan tin. Bake blind for 15 minutes. Fill the pastry case with the lemon mixture.

For the meringue; whip the egg whites until they hold their shape, add 5 oz (140 grams)/⅝ cup of the sugar and beat for another minute. (the mixture should be stiff and shiny). Lastly fold in the remaining 3 oz (85 grams)/⅜ cup of sugar until all is incorporated. Pipe this over the lemon mixture. Cook at 375°F/190°C/Regulo 5 for 10 minutes.

Galley Cruising Restaurants,
New Ross,
Co. Wexford.

Aherne's Seafood Bar.

An 18th century pub and grocery store converted into a restaurant in 1969 and extended in 1984. Near the great church of St. Mary's and some of the oldest houses in Ireland.

O utside, Ahernes is a vintage Irish Pub. Inside it is a world class Seafood Bar and restaurant. Situated in the seaport town of Youghal (pronounced 'Yawl') it is run by Gerry Fitzgibbon, his wife Betty and their sons John and David. It started as a bar, serving bar food, and grew in stature and dimension to become locally and internationally acclaimed. The Los Angeles Times called it ecstatically "One of the best seafood restaurants in the world". Food is still served in the bar as well as in the newly added restaurant. One thing is guaranteed – whichever one you choose, your meal will be a long remembered pleasure.

Aherne's Hot Potato & Smoked Salmon Starter.

6 medium sized cooked potatoes.
6 oz (170 grams) sliced, smoked salmon.
6 oz (170 grams)/1 1/3 cups grated cheese.
½ pint (300 ml)/1¼ cups cream.
Freshly ground black pepper.
Salt.
1½ oz (45 grams)/3 tblspns garlic butter.
Juice of 1 lemon.

Grease 6 3 inch (7.5 cm) ramekin dishes with garlic butter. Thinly slice cold potato and layer the bottom of the dish. Place the smoked salmon on top and season with black pepper and lemon juice. Put another layer of potato on top and cover with grated cheese. Pour cream over and bake in a hot oven for 10 minutes or until nicely browned. Garnish with a sprig of parsley.

Sea Bass baked in Orange Juice and White Wine.

6-6 oz (170 grams) fillets of Sea Bass.
Juice of 10 oranges.
1/3 bottle dry white wine.
6 bay leaves.
6 sprigs of fennel.
Olive oil.

Coat 6 flat oven-proof dishes with olive oil. Place a fillet of fish in each dish and season with freshly ground black pepper. Pour over orange juice and wine and add a bay-leaf and sprig of fennel to each dish. Bake in a hot oven for approx 20 minutes.

Aherne's Seafood Bar,
163 North Main Street,
Youghal,
Co. Cork.

Blairs Cove

The house was built in 1720 and remodelled by Philippe and Sabine De Mey in 1981. The barn is now a double height structure of stripped stone dominated by a tiered fireplace based on a Swiss prototype to grill, smoke and mull, contrasting to the chandeliers and furniture from the De Mey family home in Bruges.

Blairs Cove, a Georgian mansion with adjoining cottages which have been converted into self catering houses and flats. The main stable building in the 250 year old stable yard has been stunningly converted into a stylish restaurant. Just to eat at Blairs makes a trip to Ireland worth while.

Smoked Salmon Mousse.

8 fl. oz (250 ml)/1 cup milk (boiled).
8 fl. oz (250 ml)/1 cup cream.
4 egg yolks.
10½ oz (300 grams) trimmings of smoked salmon (or ½ fresh salmon).
5 gelatine leaves.
Few slices salmon for mould.

Oil mould and cover bottom with a thin layer of smoked salmon. Blend salmon in a food processor. Whisk egg yolks shortly in small saucepan and pour the boiled milk over. Stir with wooden spoon and add soaked gelatine leaves and allow this mixture to cool (e.g. in a cold water bath). As soon as the mixture starts setting, mix with smoked salmon, blend in whipped cream thoroughly and fill the mould. Let cool in fridge for a minimum of 2 hours, unmould onto a platter and serve immediately.

Escalopes of Veal Stuffed with Sweetbreads in a Mushroom Cream Sauce.

3 escalopes.
Farce:–
3½ fl. oz (100 mls)/⅜ cup cream.
3 egg whites, (chilled).
Pepper/salt.
9 oz. (250 grams) sweetbreads, poached.
Mushrooms.

Put escalopes into a food processor and purée. Set aside. In a basin beat the egg whites, add the cream and season with pepper and salt. Fold in sweetbreads which have been previously plucked apart. Season your escalopes and fold them over a large tblspn of farce. Fry them in butter. When nearly done, add mushroom slices. Remove meat and finish sauce as follows: Add some homemade stock, and cream, reduce until slightly thick. Check the seasoning and serve.

Almond Roll.

10 eggs.
9 oz (250 grams)/1⅛ cups sugar.
9 oz (250 grams)/1¾ cups flour.

Beat sugar and eggs until pale, fold in flour gradually. Spread on a baking tray on greaseproof paper and bake at 400°F/200°C/Reg 6 for 10 minutes. Take out of oven and place immediately between two dampened cloths.

Almond Filling.

2 oz (55 grams)/¼ cup sugar.
1 dessertspn water.
3 egg yolks.
4 leaves of gelatine.
3½ oz (100 grams)/½ cup Quark or cottage cheese.
4 oz (110 grams)/½ cup cream.
1 dessertspn sugar.
A few drops almond essence.

Boil water and sugar for two minutes to make syrup. Allow to cool a little and then beat together with the egg yolks into a mousse. Add soaked gelatine and Quark or cottage cheese while the mixture is still warm. Whip the cream together with the dessertspn of sugar and almond essence. Fold into the above mixture, then spread it out on the sponge and roll up.

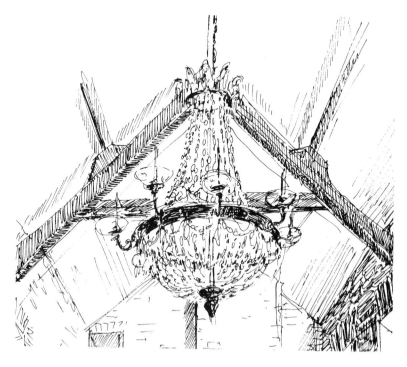

Blairs Cove Restaurant,
Durrus,
Nr Bantry,
Co. Cork.

120

MacCloskeys

Bunratty House was built in 1804 by Thomas Studdert of Bunratty Castle. It was intended as a temporary home until he inherited the castle. However as Bunratty House was more comfortable than the nearby castle, Thomas Studdert stayed put and the castle became a ruin. MacCloskey's Restaurant is in the basement of this house.

To get into MacCloskey's you descend a staircase into a basement built into the side of a hill. A series of little vaulted cellar rooms offer views through tiny windows over the roof-tops of Bunratty Folk Park and the battlements of the castle. Each little white washed dining room accommodates 6-8 tables and one doesn't get the feeling of dining in an ordinary crowded restaurant. The meals are quite splendid with the most perfectly cooked and served vegetables. Halfway between Shannon airport and Limerick city, this very special restaurant has a marvellous address. Bunratty Castle for a neighbour and the Folk Park arrayed around it.

Devilled Crab Cakes with Tarragon Sauce.

6 oz (170 grams)/¾ cup butter.
½ green pepper, finely chopped.
4 oz (110 grams)/1 cup onion, finely chopped.
½ pimento, chopped.
1 tspn salt.
½ tspn pepper.
1 tspn thyme.
1 tblspn Worcestershire sauce.
Few drops tabasco.
12 oz (340 grams) white crabmeat.
1 egg.
Flour, to dust cakes.

Coating
2 eggs and 4 fl. oz. (120 ml)/½ cup milk beaten together,
Fine cracker crumbs, to roll cakes in.

Melt butter in a saucepan over a low heat. In it sweat pepper, onion and pimento for approx 25 minutes. Add salt, pepper, thyme, Worcestershire and tabasco sauce. Cook for a further 10 minutes, stirring occasionally. Stir in crab meat. Remove from heat and allow to cool. Whisk the egg and stir into the mixture.

Using a small round pastry cutter, cut into 1" (2.5 cm) cakes. Dust with flour and refrigerate for 15 minutes.

Dip the cakes in the egg and milk mixture, and roll in fine cracker crumbs. Pre-heat oven to 360°F/180°C/Regulo 4. Heat 1" (2.5cm) of cooking oil in a deep pan to 360°F/180-190°C. Lower cakes in and deep fry for 1 minute on each side or until brown. Drain on absorbent paper. Bake in oven for 10-15. Serve immediately.

Tarragon Sauce.

Skin and bones of fish. (e.g. salmon, sole, etc.)
12 tarragon leaves chopped.
5 fl. oz. (150 ml)/⅝ cup cream.
3 oz (85 grams)/6 tblspns butter.
1 tspn parsley, chopped.
Salt & pepper.
Lemon juice.

Put skin and fish bones in a saucepan with 10 fl.oz/300 ml/1¼ cups water. Cover and simmer for 25 minutes. Strain into another saucepan and boil hard until liquid is reduced to 2 tblspns. Add tarragon and parsley, cover and cook for 1-2 minutes. Reserve this residue. Melt ½ oz/15 grams/1 tblspn butter. Add half the cream and the reserved liquid. Bring to the boil and add remaining cream. Whisk in the rest of the butter piece by piece over a gentle heat. Do not allow sauce to boil. Season with salt, pepper and lemon juice. Serve crab cakes on a warm plate in a pool of hot tarragon sauce.

Veal Steaks with Lemon.

6-8 oz (170-225 grams) veal per steak.

Pare julienne strips of lemon peel from half a lemon. Put into a saucepan of cold water, bring to the boil and drain. Put in a saucepan with a soupspn of water and a touch of sugar. Remove from heat when the water has evaporated and the julienne is a brilliant colour. Season the veal fillets and colour on both sides in a pan of heated butter. Remove the veal and set on a warm plate. Tip out the cooking butter, pour in 4 soupspns of dry white wine and reduce by 2/3 over a low flame. Whisk in 1 oz (30 grams)/2 tblspns butter to make an emulsion and add a tspn chopped parsley. Season with salt and pepper. Pour the juices from the fillets into the sauce and coat the fillets. Garnish each fillet with a slice of lemon (without peel) and a pinch of the lemon julienne. Serve with a risotto or some vegetables cooked in butter.

Fresh Strawberry Soufflé.

1¼ oz (35 grams)/2½ tblspns butter.
3 tblspns flour.
2 tblspns castor sugar.
10 fl. oz (300 ml)/1¼ cups cream (scalded).
5 eggs (separated).
6 oz (170 grams) strawberries, (chopped and hulled).

Melt the butter gently in a saucepan. Add the flour and cook for 2 minutes to make a blonde roux. Gradually add the scalded cream and cook over a low heat for 3-4 minutes. Whisk egg yolks and castor sugar until pale. Remove saucepan from heat and stir in egg mixture. Chop strawberries roughly, and fold into soufflé mixture. Butter 6 individual soufflé dishes and dust with castor sugar. Whisk egg whites until stiff and lightly fold into mixture. Turn into prepared dishes and cook in a pre-heated oven at 450°F/250°C/Regulo 9 for 10 minutes or until puffed and brown on top. Decorate with sifted icing sugar and slices of strawberries. Serve immediately.

MacCloskey's Restaurant,
Bunratty House Mews,
Co. Clare.

Doyle's Seafood Restaurant.

A small village shop and pub built in 1790. It has its original range and slate floor. Restored by Stella and John Doyle in 1968 and extended by them to accomodate the present restaurant. The recent acquisition of the adjoining house by Doyles will extend their operation into an hotel in 1988. The eight suites planned will be in sympathy with the style of the old building.

The drive from Killarney to Dingle is a tarmac roller-coaster that twists and turns along the shores of the Dingle Peninsula. The uncluttered beauty of the scenery improves with every bump and bend. At journey's end is Doyle's Seafood Bar, *the* place for excellent seafood.

John Doyle was a commercial off shore fisherman in Dingle when Stella started her seafood bar. With their combined expertise it thrived from early days. Stella has used the off season break to study in some of the great kitchens in France and returned to upgrade and upmarket Doyle's. John eventually gave up fishing to concentrate on the restaurant. I spent two enthralling hours listening to the Doyles talking fish and fish cooking and saw their stainless steel, heat controlled salt water tank in the "out-back" where they store the daily catches of shellfish. John's knowledge of the fishermen and their fish ensures a great variety of the best fish– on your plate the day it is caught. The impressive wine list includes Californian, Australian and European vintages. As a sop to non-fish eaters they have a meat dish on their menu.

Scallop Mousse with Beurre Blanc Sauce.

6 oz (170 grams) scallops.
1 egg.
4 fl. oz (120 ml)/½ cup light cream.
1 tblspn softened butter.
Salt, pepper, nutmeg.

Pre-heat oven to 425°F/220°C/Regulo 7. Put the scallops, a pinch of salt, ground pepper and nutmeg in a food processor. Mix thoroughly, add the egg. Allow mixer to turn once or twice, pour in the cream rapidly and then stop mixer. The ingredients should be cold. Butter the ramekin dishes and fill with the mousse. Place the ramekins in a dish of warm water and put into a pre-heated oven for 20 minutes.

Beurre Blanc Sauce.

5 fl. oz (150 ml)/¼ pint white wine.
Black pepper corns.
Sprig parsley.
Bay-leaf.
1 tblspn light cream.
4 oz (110 grams)/½ cup butter.

In a heavy or copper saucepan put the wine, whole pepper, parsley and bay leaf. Reduce down to about 1 tblspn of liquid. Add the cream. Let it boil to thicken slightly. Whisk in the butter in pieces. Season to taste.

Brown Trout with Mushroom Sauce.

4 oz (110 grams)/½ cup butter.
3 oz (85 grams)/approx ⅝ cup flour.
6 trout.
12 mushrooms.
5 fl. oz (150 ml)/⅝ cup fish stock.
10 fl. oz (300 ml)/1¼ cups sour cream.
1 tspn lemon juice.
1 tspn paprika.
Salt & pepper.

Rinse the mushrooms. Place in a pan with the butter. Cook for about 10 minutes or until there is plenty of juice with the mushrooms. Add paprika and flour. Cook for a further few minutes. Add the stock, salt and pepper. Lastly add the sour cream and lemon juice. Bake the trout in a hot oven for about 12 minutes. Serve with the sauce.

Pear Cake.

Ingredients for sponge base:

3 oz (85 grams)/6 tblspns butter.
3 oz (85 grams)/1/3 cup sugar.
1 egg.
3oz (85 grams)/approx ⅝ cup self-raising flour.

Ingredients for pear topping:

16 oz (450 grams) tin of pears, (drained).
7 leaves gelatine.
13 oz (390 ml)/1½ cups whipped cream.
2 egg whites, (whisked).
4 tblspns Poire William liqueur.

To make sponge:

Put the first 4 ingredients into a food processor and beat. Put into an 8 inch (20 cm) lined and greased sponge tin. Cook at 350°F/180°C/Regulo 4, for 20 minutes. Leave to cool. Cut in half horizontally. Put into a loose bottomed 8 inch (20 cm) tin and pour pear mixture on top.

To make topping:

Melt the gelatine in a little warm water. Add to puréed pears, with the Poire William, whipped cream and whisked egg whites. Pour over the sponge and leave to set.

Doyle's Seafood Bar,
John Street,
Dingle,
Co. Kerry.

Drimcong House Restaurant

Original 17th century lakeside house just outside Galway remodelled in 18th century. It has exceptionally fine carved stone Queen Anne doorcase. Owned and run as a restaurant by Gerry and Marie Galvin.

In the Galway area, you couldn't do better than seek out Drimcong House. With a skilled menu, expertly executed, it is one of those wonderful and unique places that one could hardly fault. In the kitchen Gerry Galvin presents his platters like rare works of art, and even if you sit down with the best "must watch my weight" attitude, I defy you to keep it up beyond the first ounce (28 grams!) of the first course.

Mussels in a Lettuce Sauce.

1 dozen plump mussels per person.
1 cup of "Lambs" lettuce.
2 oz (55 grams)/4 tblspns unsalted butter.
½ pint (300 ml)/1¼ cups cream.
¼ pint (150 ml)/⅝ cup mussel liquor.
White pepper.

Steam and shell mussels and keep warm. Combine lettuce and butter in a food processor until amalgamated. Keep chilled. Reduce cream and mussel liquor over high heat for 3 minutes. Reduce heat, add butter and whisk until incorporated in the cream. Add mussels and serve with a pinch or two of white pepper.
N.B. Salt should not be used at any stage in this recipe.

Roast Pheasant & Game "Jus".

6 oven-ready pheasants with legs removed.
1 pint (600 ml)/2½ cups game stock.
1 tblspn sherry vinegar.
1 tblspn finely chopped shallot.
¼ pint (150 ml)/⅝ cup red wine.
Hazelnut oil.
Seasoning.

Make a mousse with the leg meat, a little egg white and whipped cream. Put in "Timbale" moulds and chill. Over high heat cook shallot, wine, and vinegar until syrupy. Add stock and reduce briskly for ten minutes, when the "jus" should be gamey and flavoursome. Season if necessary. In a hot oven, roast seasoned pheasants in hazelnut oil for 20 minutes, turning once. At the same time bake the "timbales" for the same duration, in a bain-marie. Unmould the timbales, remove and carve breasts, and serve together with hot "jus".

Avocado Sorbet.

3 medium avocados.
Juice of 1 lemon.
1 tblspn honey.
1 tblspn vodka.
Salt and white pepper.
1 egg white.

Peel and chop avocado and toss in a mixture of lemon juice, honey, vodka, salt and pepper. Liquidise. Incorporate beaten egg white and process in an ice-cream machine or sorbetière. Store in freezer and allow to soften a little before use. Decorate with herbs or flowers such as borage or lemon balm.

Drimcong House Restaurant,
Moycullen,
Co. Galway.

Dunderry Lodge Restaurant

The original farm dates from 1850. The byre and barn have been converted into a very striking restaurant by Nicholas and Catherine Healy.

Pheasant Solferino.

3 Pheasants.
3 oz (85 grams) Chicken Liver Pâté.
3 tblspns dry Dubonnet.
8 fl. oz (250 ml)/1 cup cream.
Roasted almonds & parsley to garnish.

Lift the skin from the breast of each pheasant and using a palette knife spread the paté over the flesh of each bird. Place the pheasants in a roasting dish, add the dry Dubonnet and seasoning, cover with tin foil and cook at 425°F (220°C)/Reg 7 for 30 minutes. Remove the tin foil and strain off all the juices into a small saucepan. Return the pheasants to the oven for approximately 10 minutes or until nicely browned. Add the cream to the juices in the saucepan and reduce until the sauce is thick and shiny, season to taste. Carve the pheasants into 6 portions, pour the sauce over and garnish with roasted almonds and parsley.

Country Terrine.

1 lb (450 grams) belly of pork.
4 oz (110 grams) pork liver.
4 oz (110 grams) sausage meat.
4 oz (110 grams) streaky bacon.
1 clove garlic.
¼ large Golden Delicious apple
3 juniper berries.
2 sage leaves.
1 tblspn Cinzano Rosso.
Salt and black pepper.

Chop the bacon into small pieces. Peel and core the apple. Peel and crush the garlic. Mince all the other meat coarsely with the apple. Mix all together in a large bowl with the chopped bacon, crushed garlic, chopped sage leaves and crushed juniper berries. Add salt, black pepper and the Cinzano Rosso. Pour mixture into a porcelain terrine dish, place in a bain marie, cover and bake at 300°F/150°C/Reg 2 for 2 hours. Cool with a weight on top of the terrine. Do not use for at least 24 hours.

Honey and Lavender Icecream.

1 tblspn dried lavender.
2 tblspns honey.
1 pint (600 ml)/2½ cups cream.
1 pint (600 ml)/2½ cups custard.

Make an infusion with the lavender and 2 tblspns water. Strain carefully into a small bowl, add the honey and mix together. Add to the cream and custard and freeze in an icecream machine.

Dunderry Lodge Restaurant,
Dunderry,
Navan,
Co. Meath.

Architectural Notes

The country houses and restaurants illustrated here represent a narrow cross section of Irish domestic architecture, but they suggest a solution to the conservation of the remainder .

Few historic houses can survive on their takings at the door. They may provide the owners with their supper but cannot mend the roof. Open in this way they are so often empty shells; but when they open their doors to guests, offering four poster beds, as well as fish and game served by candle light, they spring to life again with their visitors no longer voyeurs but participators. They are not only preserved, but enjoyed.

Why then has this association received so little recognition in Ireland, so much at variance with their success abroad? They pre-date Official Tourism with their sources in either Edwardian shooting lodges of the West, or in the lush farmlands and walled gardens of Munster. Since they were never standardised in the 1960's they require to be treated with special sensitivity by who ever is in charge of the local bye laws. They are remarkable in the resourcefulness and independent-mindedness of each proprietor. Twenty-five of the owners are their own architects, nearly all tend their own gardens and organise their own interior decoration while at least three houses contain large collections of paintings by close relatives. Among the paintings, there is occasionally a tribute from a guest, a record of an afternoon's enchantment.

The drawings in this book are in that tradition. They are portraits of houses. What I have stressed is not so much the architecture as their inner ambience and outward setting. So many of these houses are sited over water that magically reflects them. Only having captured it by balancing precariously over a very strong and cold November current, can one appreciate the original skill of the builder in linking house to landscape.

Jeremy Williams

133

Pheasant
Pheasant Solferino 131
Roast Pheasant and Game Jus 128

Pigeon
Pigeon Breast
with Lime and Peppery Pineapple 112
Pigeon Breast Gelée 14
Pigeon Pie 104
Salade de Pigeon 18

Pike Quenelles 100

Fresh Prawns en Croûte
with Provençale Sauce 66

Prawn Puffs
with side salad and Ohio Sauce 96

Salmon
Aherne's Hot Potato
and Smoked Salmon Starter 117
Darne de Saumon
aux Pointes D'Asperges 18
Fillet of Salmon Mousseline 42
Gravad Lax 74
Poached Salmon 93
Smoked Salmon Mousse 119
Terrine of Smoked Salmon 54

Scallop Mousse
with Beurre Blanc Sauce 125

Sea Bass baked in Orange Juice
and white wine 117

Seafood Pâté 58

Sauces
Avocado 50
Beurre Blanc 125
Caramel 59
Francatelli 100
Hollandaise 42
Juniper Berry 34
Lemon 54
Mint Hollandaise 89
Mulled Wine 96
Ohio 96
Provençale 66
Pinekernel 34
Tarragon 123
Fresh Tomato 34
White Wine 47
Yoghurt and Herb 70

Soufflé
Fresh Strawberry 123
Irish Mist 23

Soups
Broccili with Garlic Croûtons 70
Carrot and Onion Soup 104
Carrot and Orange Soup 78
Galley Tomato and Mint Soup 115
Lettuce and Mint Soup 22
Mulligatawny Soup 62
Potato and Ham Soup 10

Swan Lake Meringues 11

Tarts
Fluffy Almond Tart 43
Tarte au Citron 18-19
Treacle Tart 75

Terrines
Country Terrine 131
Game Terrine
with Gooseberry Chutney 46
Smoked Salmon Terrine 54

Tomatoes
Tomatoe Icecream with Prawns 82

Trout
Brown Trout
with Mushroom Sauce 126
Hot Smoked Trout
with Yoghurt and Herb Sauce 70

Veal
Baked Stuffed Leg of Veal
with Lemon Sauce 54
Escalopes of Veal stuffed
with sweetbreads in a Mushroom 119
Cream Sauce
Veal Haxe on Mirepoix 38
Veal Steaks with Lemon 123